T0318237

Theorizing the Resilience of American Higher Education

This book proposes a new theory of change in American higher education that explains the resilience of colleges and universities, and demonstrates how they adapt to new social and economic conditions. It argues that the demands for new educational missions, new sources of capital to finance innovation, and new organizational and governance models lead to the creation of institutional diversity. Using the theory of "accretive change" to predict future changes, this volume asserts that the rise of artificial intelligence and new investment models within the field of social entrepreneurship will shape the next wave of universities and educational institutions.

Geoffrey M. Cox is the Senior Associate Dean for Administration and Finance, and Lecturer at the Stanford University Graduate School of Education, USA.

Theorizing the Resilience of American Higher Education

How Colleges and Universities Adapt to Changing Social and Economic Conditions

Geoffrey M. Cox

Routledge
Taylor & Francis Group
New York London

First published 2019
by Routledge
52 Vanderbilt Avenue, New York, NY 10017

and by Routledge
2 Park Square, Milton Park, Abingdon, Oxon, OX14 4RN

First issued in paperback 2020

Routledge is an imprint of the Taylor & Francis Group, an informa business

Library of Congress Cataloguing-in-Publication Data
Names: Cox, Geoffrey Mark, 1955– author.
Title: Theorizing the resilience of American higher education : how
    colleges and universities adapt to changing social and economic
    conditions/by Geoffrey M. Cox.
Description: New York : Routledge, [2019] | Includes bibliographical
    references.
Identifiers: LCCN 2019010002 | ISBN 9780367226992 (hardback) |
    ISBN 9780429276446 (ebook)
Subjects: LCSH: Universities and colleges—United States—
    Administration. Universities and colleges—United States—Finance. |
    Education, Higher—Aims and objectives—United States. |
    Organizational change—United States. | Artificial intelligence—
    Educational applications.
Classification: LCC LB2341 .C834 2019 | DDC 378.1/01—dc23
LC record available at https://lccn.loc.gov/2019010002

ISBN 13: 978-0-367-67177-8 (pbk)
ISBN 13: 978-0-367-22699-2 (hbk)

Typeset in Times New Roman
by Apex CoVantage, LLC

For Greg, my brother

Contents

Tables

Acknowledgements

I am grateful to many friends and colleagues who have supported my forays into the study of higher education. This includes generous teachers, mentors, and colleagues too numerous to name individually. Among them, however, Derrick Anderson, Patricia Gumport, and Mitchell Stevens read an early draft of the main thesis and encouraged me to continue developing it. I thank them in particular for their interest in my efforts.

I am also grateful to my colleagues at Stanford's Graduate School of Education, and especially to its Dean, Dan Schwartz. They, and he, have created the most congenial working environment I've known over the course of a forty-year career in higher education.

Special thanks go to Caitlin Brust for her many helpful substantive and editorial suggestions in the final stages, and for her tenacious pursuit of wayward references and citations.

Any sustained writing project requires a fair amount of woolgathering. My family indulges me in this, for which I'm also thankful.

Part I

1 Commencing

It is a warm spring day, and the campus has been carefully manicured to look its best. Families stroll the grounds, visibly filled with a mixture of pride, happiness, and perhaps relief that this day has finally come. Their graduating daughters and sons meet the day with mixed emotions as well. They, too, are proud to have finally arrived at this turning point in life, but they are apprehensive about the prospect of leaving the familiar, supportive community in which they have lived for four years. Perhaps they are anxious about the future, or eager to get on with it, or some combination of both. It is, for everyone concerned, one of those few moments in life in which something important changes. A milestone is passed, a fork in the road is taken, a passage is completed, a page is turned. What would graduation day be without clichés?

It has been my privilege to participate in a great many commencement ceremonies over the span of more than forty years—as a student, as a parent, and as the president or senior staff member of several institutions. I have processed into the University of Chicago's somber, majestic Rockefeller Chapel to receive a doctorate degree, and I have marched into Stanford's football stadium in cap and gown alongside bizarrely costumed students participating in the irreverent annual Wacky Walk. Having also served as president of an institution with academic programs in four countries, I have presided over commencements in locations as diverse as Hong Kong, Tokyo, and Mexico City. There is nothing quite like marching in cap and gown to music from a mariachi band!

I consider myself fortunate to have experienced commencement as an annual ritual in my personal and professional life. I still get goosebumps at the sight of the faculty marching two-by-two in their colorful academic regalia. I am proud to put on my own maroon robe and hood trimmed in dark blue, which, to initiates of the academic code, signals the institution from which I earned my doctorate degree and the discipline (Philosophy) that I studied.

The traditional commencement pageant is academia's most visible connection to its medieval origins. Most histories of Western higher education begin with the founding of the University of Bologna in the year 1088. The European universities established in that era, including Oxford, Cambridge, and Paris, were closely aligned with the church, and today's commencement ceremony is most fully understood as a secular liturgy. The caps and gowns are clerical in their origins, and the hooding ceremony for new doctors of the academy echoes the laying on of hands that creates new priests and bishops. The conferral of degrees formally occurs only at the moment when the university president pronounces a ritualized sentence, not unlike the administration of sacraments such as baptism and marriage.[1] The academic parade itself is an analogue of a liturgical procession, with candidates for degrees (i.e., religious novitiates) leading the way, followed by the faculty (priests), and finally the senior hierarchy of the institution; the university president brings up the rear in place of the bishop or most senior celebrant. These symbols are scarcely recognized by most graduates and families at modern commencements, but they resonate over nearly a thousand years of history. As in the church, the entire ceremony is intended to inspire awe, mystery, and respect.

My pride in participating in these ceremonies over many years stems from my affection for universities and their long history; I am an academic romantic at heart. And yet, I have often found myself observing the commencement ceremony with bemused curiosity. How is that this highly stylized ritual has survived for so long, and is replicated in places so far from its origins? How much of the commencement ceremony that we practice today would have been recognizable to our academic predecessors from previous centuries? Why do we think that this particular form of pageantry retains its authority and appeal in a modern society that otherwise has little reverence for history and ceremony?

Some of the most familiar aspects of the modern commencement ceremony are in fact relatively recent innovations. For example, the codification of academic regalia (i.e. different colored gowns and hoods representing specific institutions and disciplines, respectively) began to take shape in 1895 when a group of U.S. institutions met to agree to some common rules, but wasn't fully formalized until 1932 when the American Council on Education decided to lend its authority to the matter (American Council on Education, 2018). The custom of shifting the tassel on one's mortarboard from right to left at the end of the ceremony is prescribed nowhere, but has in recent years become a firm part of the tradition at some institutions, so much so that I was criticized once when I, as president, neglected to tell the graduates that they could move their tassels at the end of the ceremony. Celebrity commencement speakers are certainly a phenomenon of our star-struck times, as is the practice of awarding them honorary degrees as part of their compensation for appearing. Even the universal soundtrack of graduation processions—Elgar's Pomp and Circumstance—achieved that status only after it was first played at Yale's commencement in 1905 and began to spread among other institutions after that (Duddleston, 2016). Many of the trappings we most associate with graduations are not of medieval origin, nor ecclesiastical, nor even European, but instead are American variations on an old set of themes.

For all of the dignity and formality of the commencement ceremony, it has always had a rowdy undercurrent as well. The old graduation hymn *Gaudeamus Igitur* (*Now Let Us Rejoice*) is a bawdy drinking song dressed up as a sentimental ode to college days. At many institutions today, graduates feel free to decorate their regalia with sequins, dollar bills, and just about anything else that can be glued to a mortarboard. Pity the poor commencement speaker whose charge is to inspire a moment of reflection about the significance of the day, but who must sometimes compete with beach balls bouncing through the crowd. Graduation day is a study in contrast: a blend of the ancient and quasi-sacred, on the one hand, and youthful energy and irreverence on the other.

The commencement ceremony is an appropriate metaphor for modern higher education in general. Today's colleges and universities are deeply rooted in a long and continuous history, and for this reason they can appear out of place in a fast-paced society in which history seems to mean little more than the most recent news cycle. To many, including plenty of the students and faculty who populate their campuses, the ways of these institutions often seem to be mysteriously archaic, if not at times ridiculous. At the same time, many things that we most associate with academic life are relatively recent additions. Faculty tenure; shared governance among trustees, administrators, and faculty; semester units and transfer credits; undergraduate majors; and even the idea of doing basic scientific research on campus are all relatively modern inventions, many of which originated in American institutions in the early twentieth century (Davidson, 2017).

This mixture of old and new characterizes the public's perception of higher education as well. A college or university degree is one of the highest goals of modern life, and something to which students and families devote enormous energy and resources to achieve. Institutions of higher education are integral parts of an elaborate social system that identifies, cultivates, and rewards talent, and yet the institutions themselves are often seen as being isolated from the very society for which they are preparing the next generation of leaders. The most iconic images of these institutions—from the leafy campuses to the eccentric professors—seem to be extravagant anachronisms, yet they remain central to our belief in progress.

We live in a time of decreasing confidence in institutions of all kinds, and universities have not been exempt from this trend. Recent public polls (Pew Research Center, 2018) suggest growing dissatisfaction with higher education, especially among political conservatives who tend to see campuses as effete training grounds for liberals. Those with a sense of both history and irony will recall that it has been just fifty years since university campuses were rocked by violent protests instigated by liberal students who thought their institutions were too closely allied with "the establishment," to recall a word then in vogue (Horowitz, 1986). Contrary to both of these caricatures, most large universities are sufficiently diverse and multi-faceted that they typically house a broad range of political views; on most campuses one can find free-market fundamentalists in the Economics department working alongside die-hard socialists in the humanities. Although academic respect for free speech has come under severe pressure in our polarized times, large university campuses remain among the few enduring institutions where one might have even hope of finding serious diversity of opinion and genuine exchanges of ideas. The academic enterprise also includes many institutions that are more homogenous by design, but among these there is also broad diversity, ranging from those that are formally committed to religious fundamentalism and political conservatism to others that seem only to attract secular liberals. This cacophony within the ranks of higher education is bound to disappoint critics on both ends of the political spectrum, who would prefer to see the prestige of the academy unequivocally on their preferred side of every political question.

Beyond these political critiques, higher education is buffeted by anxieties about technology, globalization, and other forces that seem to have escaped our control. We are told by pundits and futurists that most of the jobs we hold today are set to vanish within a generation, that robotics and artificially intelligent machines will increasingly displace us, that our personal and private identities are mere data points in a ubiquitous cloud of information that is subject to exploitation by the digital elite, and that the cultures and traditions that have long bound communities together are being swept aside in a vast, homogenizing wave of global integration. We are also told that a college degree is more critical than ever to navigating these turbulent times, but its apparent cost floats ever farther out of reach for everyone except those already at the top of the economic strata. If universities are supposed to prepare us for this future world, they do not seem up to the task. If they are keepers of our traditions and values, they seem derelict in their duty. If they are gatekeepers to the good life, they seem to be failing many of those who most need help getting there.

As a result of these criticisms and anxieties, it has become increasingly common to hear that colleges and universities are dinosaurs—out of touch with the contemporary environment and too slow to move and change. Some commentators seem sad but resigned to the apparently inevitable decline and fall of higher education, while others can barely conceal their glee. Ambitious attempts to "disrupt" the established academic order attract talented entrepreneurs and big-time investments. Politicians score rhetorical points by lambasting out-of-touch elitists on college campuses, while they steadily whittle away at public funding for both institutions and students. In the face of such criticism, the higher education community seems at times unable to explain itself, much less defend its principles and purposes.

This is not entirely new, nor, in my view, does it herald the imminent demise of colleges and universities. Campus life has long been the object of parody and criticism, especially given the persistent anti-intellectual streak that runs through the American polity (Hofstadter, 1963). Higher education has, from time to time, needed an infusion of new ideas in order to bring itself into line with the needs and demands of society. The thesis of this book is a simple one: higher education has been remarkably adept at changing with the times, and there is no reason to think that this capacity has been lost. I propose to develop an argument in support of this position in two parts. In Part One, I will show that American higher education has gone through periods of rapid innovation at fairly frequent intervals, especially since the Civil War. These periods of change have been marked by three factors in the external environment: new social demands on colleges and universities; the availability of capital from new sources to finance innovation; and the emergence of new organizational models that can be adapted to academic goals. These external forces have been met with and matched by changes in the internal environments of colleges and universities, characterized by new academic missions, new business models, and new ways of organizing authority and control. These are the adaptive mechanisms of individual colleges and universities. From a systemic perspective, higher education has been unusual in the extent to which innovations have spread through informal networks of cooperation and emulation across organizational types. Thus, the diversity of forms that allows for different adaptive responses persists, benefiting all parts of the system and not just innovative newcomers. In this respect, higher education, with its collegial culture, differs from winner-take-all systems such as those often found in business and industry.

Part Two of this book is more speculative, but I intend to show that it is nonetheless grounded in the same theory of change that we can discover by looking back in time. I will argue that the three dynamics of change that we have seen in the past will re-occur, and with broadly foreseeable results. What we can reasonably surmise is that innovation will continue with respect to academic missions, organizational structures, and methods of financing. As in the past, innovative institutions will arise in response to new demands on the higher education system, but they are unlikely to displace most older organizations or institutional forms. Instead, some of the innovations developed by new institutions will be adopted and refined by incumbent colleges and universities. While there will be casualties along the way—institutions that cannot keep pace with the need for change or that fail to respond to environmental cues—the mainstream of higher education will continue to flow into the future.

As I have already admitted, I am a romantic about the traditions of academia, but I hope to avoid being naively optimistic. Higher education must change if it is to continue to be relevant to society. My contention is that the capacity for change is built into the loosely knit fabric of the higher education system, especially in the United States. If there is an even simpler way to formulate my premise, it is by inverting a familiar catchphrase: the more things stay the same, the more they will change. In other words, change has been and will continue to be a constant in higher education. The plan of this book is to show how this strategy has worked in the past—and how it is likely to continue working in the near future.

Note

1. Austin (1955/1976) calls these ritualized phrases "performatives" because they are a special class of sentences that actually change facts about the world when they are said under the right circumstances. When the officiant at a wedding says, "I now pronounce you husband and wife," something of legal, social, and moral significance happens in that instant. The same kind of thing occurs when a judge says "I find you guilty." In the case of graduation, the usual formula is: "I now confer upon you the degree of X, with all of the rights and privileges pertaining thereto," or something similar.

Bibliography

Austin, J. (1955/1976). *How to do thing with words*. Cambridge: Harvard University Press.

Brown, A. (2018). *Most Americans see higher ed as heading the wrong direction, but partisans disagree on why*. Washington, DC: Pew Research Center. Retrieved from www.pewresearch.org/fact-tank/2018/07/26/most-americans-say-higher-ed-is-heading-in-wrong-direction-but-partisans-disagree-on-why/

Davidson, C. (2017). *The new education: How to revolutionize the university to prepare students for a world in flux*. New York: Basic Books.

Duddleston, M. (2016, May 23). *Graduation and Elgar's "Pomp and Circumstance": What's the connection?* Retrieved from www.wrti.org/post/graduation-and-elgars-pomp-and-circumstance-whats-connection

Hofstadter, R. (1963). *Anti-intellectualism in American life*. New York: Knopf.

Horowitz, H. (1986). The 1960s and the transformation of campus culture. In *History of education quarterly* (Vol. 26, No. 1, pp. 1–38). Cambridge: Cambridge University Press.

Sullivan, E. (1997/2018). *Historical overview of the academic costume code*. American Council on Education, reprinted with permission from American Universities and Colleges (15th ed.). Walter de Gruyter, Inc. Retrieved from www.acenet.edu/news-room/Pages/Historical-Overview-Academic-Costume-Code.aspx

2   Institutional Longevity

In this book, I seek to explain how change occurs in American higher education. I will try to expose the structural features of the academic enterprise that make it remarkably adaptive to changing conditions in society and in the economy. Identifying these organizational and structural features of the American approach to higher education will also enable us to look ahead to changes that may come in the near future.

For some critics of higher education, a theory of change will seem like a strange pursuit because it is often assumed that colleges and universities change very little, if at all. They seem to occupy the same buildings, employ the same kinds of faculty members, house the same dusty books, and teach the same kinds of subjects as they always have, in some cases, for centuries. At public events, such as commencement, the faculty, students, and administrators don medieval caps and gowns as if to underscore their links to ancient academic traditions. To some observers, this suggests that higher education spends too much time admiring its own reflection in a rearview mirror. The entire academic enterprise "is beset by hubris, opposition to change, and resistance to accountability" (Selingo, 2013, p. X), according to one critic. Comparing academia to other industries that became complacent and unresponsive to change, management gurus from Peter Drucker (Lenzner & Johnson, 1997) to Clayton Christensen (Lederman, 2017, April 28) have predicted the imminent demise or disruption of colleges and universities as we now know them. Even the federal government has joined the chorus. A 2006 commission warned that the nation's higher education institutions were headed toward the fate of other mature industries that failed "to respond to—or even notice—changes in the world around them" (U.S. Department of Education, 2006, p. xii). The common thread running through these critiques is that colleges and universities are isolated from social and economic change, and structurally incapable of making the kinds of changes that would be required to keep them up to date with the demands of our times.

A very different perspective comes from a careful reading of the history of higher education. Colleges and universities played a significant role in the development and expansion of the United States, evolving along with other social and technological changes. In fact, "for the first two centuries, colleges existed in a preindustrial economy and a largely rural society. After the Civil War, they gradually adapted to an industrializing economy, an urbanizing society, and a global knowledge regime" (Geiger, 2015, p. IX). Universities were not mere bystanders through these social and economic transitions. They were often seen as instrumental to them, contributing to the expansion of knowledge and technology that fuels innovation and economic growth. Campuses grew and multiplied to help meet the demand for a more educated workforce. Discoveries in science, medicine, and technology, many of which came from university research departments, contributed to the general rise in affluence, well-being, and longevity for much of the population. For generations, policy makers, philanthropists, anxious parents, and aspiring students all accepted as self-evident the idea that higher education is both a broadly desirable public good—and a gateway to personal prosperity.

Recently, however, confidence in higher education has waned. Although most studies still conclude that the economic return from a college degree is positive, there is growing alarm about rising costs, exploding student debt loads, and the relevance of traditional education for a rapidly changing job market. Some critics argue that higher education is no longer effective as a means of rising through the economic strata, and instead now serves to reinforce structural disparities (Metzler, 2014). Other critics worry that college campuses are out of step with mainstream values, and have become centers of indoctrination into liberalism and political correctness (Deresewicz, 2017; Sullivan, 2017). There seems to be a growing backlash against the idea that higher education is intrinsically good for both individuals and the larger society.

Partly in response to these criticisms, new alternatives to traditional higher education are springing up everywhere. Online education is the most prominent innovation of the past few decades, and continues to be regarded by some as a radical threat to campus-based colleges and universities. In addition, some employers are taking a greater role in offering educational opportunities to their employees as a form of do-it-yourself workforce development. Still other kinds of businesses offer efficient, targeted training in high demand fields such as software coding without all the trappings of college. New education-related start-ups attract billions of dollars in venture funding, all based on the premise that entirely new approaches are needed.

The question before us in this book is whether academia has lost its ability to keep pace with a world that seems to be spinning faster than ever before. Have we reached the point at which the genteel traditions of higher education are costly liabilities rather than aids to progress? And, if so, what organizational structures and educational methods might take the place of traditional colleges and universities? Or, alternatively, do traditional colleges and universities have within them the ability to adapt to changing times and remain viable?

Compared to other industries, higher education is an assembly of ancient institutions. U.S. News and World Report's annual rankings for 2017 lists 311 "national universities" and 233 "national liberal arts colleges" (U.S. News and World Report, 2017). These 544 institutions represent the top tier of higher education in terms of reputation, selectivity, and resources. The great majority of them—88 percent, by my count—are more than 100 years old. In contrast, the average lifespan of a Fortune 500 corporation is less than 20 years, down from about 60 years in the 1950s according to the investment bank Credit Suisse (Mauboussin, Callahan, & Majd, 2017). Even as lifespans of commercial organizations grow shorter due to the introduction of new technologies and other innovations, colleges and universities seem to last forever.

The comparative longevity of colleges and universities is one of higher education's most distinctive features. A Carnegie Foundation study once found that of sixty-six institutions around the world that have been in continuous operation since the 1500s, sixty-two of them were universities (Donoghue, 2008). In the American context, colleges were among the first institutions founded in the early colonies, and the oldest of these continue to be among the most prominent and successful universities in the world. The youngest of the Ivy League universities—Cornell—was founded in 1865, a full century after the next youngest—Dartmouth—and two centuries after Harvard. It seems that academia has discovered a key to immortality that has remained out of the grasp of most other kinds of organizations.

One hypothesis that might explain the extraordinary longevity of colleges and universities is that they are buffered from economic forces faced by other organizations by a combination of wealth and regulatory protections. While it is true that academic institutions escape some of the rough-and-tumble of the commercial marketplace, the ivory tower stereotype is vastly oversimplified. The need to balance current revenues and expenses is, and has always been, a unique feature of American higher education. Many other countries regard universities as creatures of the state and support them fully though tax revenues or other forms of dedicated support. In the US, even public institutions operate on a mixture of (declining) direct subsidies and revenue generated from operations. As a result, "American colleges have always had to be nimble actors in a competitive market environment" according to education historian David Labaree (2017, p. 7). Contrary to

their placid images, most institutions of higher education are highly entrepreneurial. As a witty colleague of mine once said, "In the business world,
it's dog eat dog. In academia, it's just the reverse."[1]

A Tale of Two Schools

Two recent examples illustrate how the fate of institutions depends on both
market and non-market forces. The nearly simultaneous dramas engulfing
Sweet Briar College, a small not-for-profit liberal arts college, and Corinthian, a for-profit operator of more than one hundred career colleges, were
regarded by many in higher education as harbingers of the future.

In the spring of 2015, the board of trustees of Sweet Briar announced
that the college would close its doors by August of that year (O'Brien,
2016). Sweet Briar, a women's liberal arts college, was founded in 1901 in
northern Virginia. For more than a century it had served the daughters of
affluent families on an idyllic rural campus. The college owned more than
3,000 acres of land, including a 130-acre equestrian center. At the end of
its 2013 fiscal year it reported an endowment of nearly $90 million, and
charged $35,000 per year in tuition. Roughly 665 students were enrolled full
time. To all outward appearances, Sweet Briar epitomized wealth, privilege,
and isolation from the hustle of normal life. As a liberal arts school, it also
appeared to serve an academic mission that was indifferent to the external
economy. Providing a place for young women to ride horses and study arts
and literature for four years would hardly seem to be good preparation for
today's fast-paced, techno-centric workforce.

The Board's publicly stated reasons for planning to wind down operations
were based on its appraisal of the academic marketplace. After a year of
study, the trustees concluded that the college's rural setting and single-sex
program were no longer competitive. Young women wanted co-educational
campuses, and they wanted to be closer to internships and other opportunities available in urban areas. Although tuition levels were relatively high,
99% of students received financial aid, and the "discount rate"—the amount
by which nominal tuition was offset by college-funded scholarships and
grants—was rising. This, on top of modestly declining enrollments, had
reduced operating income, forcing the college to begin spending down por-
tions of its endowment to cover operating deficits.

Many small colleges were in essentially this same position in 2015, but
most boards of trustees consider it their fiduciary obligation to fight for
survival for as long as possible. Sweet Briar's announcement was unusual
because it represented a strategic retreat; a decision made in light of a sober
assessment of market conditions, but well before it was entirely necessary.
The college's balance sheet was still relatively healthy, and presumably

there were ways to leverage assets in order to buy time. Instead, Sweet Briar's leadership opted for an orderly closure on its own terms rather than waiting for the apparently inevitable day when angry creditors would be squabbling over last scraps of a bankrupt institution.

The Board's announcement created an immediate firestorm among students, alumni, and others interested in the college. Rather than viewing the decision as a bow to the inevitable, supporters of Sweet Briar argued that the decision was ill-considered and premature. Alumni immediately began organizing an effort to reverse the decision, including by taking legal action. In June of 2015, just three months after the Board's decision, Virginia's attorney general announced a settlement that amounted to a hostile takeover by the alumni group. The president was deposed and a new board was seated. The college remained open that fall, and contributions began pouring in. By December of 2017, Sweet Briar was able to announce that its debt rating had been upgraded: it had raised $44 million in new capital, and it had trimmed operating expenses by $2 million per year. Work began to re-tool the curriculum with new emphases on themes such as leadership, environmental sustainability, science and technology, and the arts. (Sweet Briar College, 2017). While enrollment in the fall of 2017 was down to 350 full-time students, the college's new president expressed confidence that Sweet Briar had a long future ahead of it.

Meanwhile, in a different corner of the academic world, another institution was confronting its own corporate mortality. Corinthian Colleges, Inc. was, at the time of its establishment in 1995, part of a new wave of innovation in higher education resulting from the confluence of opportunities in finance, technology, and education policy. The internet was emerging as a game-changing technology in many fields, and not least in higher education. Distance education, the latter-day manifestation of nineteenth-century correspondence schools, supported by aggressive telemarketing practices, propelled a few institutions to a scale that was previously unimaginable. The University of Phoenix, which originally offered mostly in-person classes in corporate office parks around the country, began to show how streamlined operations and a more corporate management structure could lead to explosive growth. Fueled by a hungry venture capital system on the lookout for "killer apps," investors were betting heavily on higher education as a lucrative new form of e-commerce. Corinthian's business model was to focus on vocational education in areas such as allied health and technology. Rather than create institutions from scratch, it bought existing ones and worked to maximize economies of scale by centralizing administration, marketing, and other overhead costs. By 2010, Corinthian operated more than one hundred sites under three "brand names:" Heald College, Wyotech Institutes, and Everest College. Tuition for a two-year degree from a Corinthian school approached $40,000. At its peak, the corporation served 110,000 students and generated annual revenues of $1.7 billion (Williams, 2016).

By 2011, enrollments began to decline in the wake of the Great Recession. It has long been conventional wisdom in higher education that it is a counter-cyclical industry. When the economy slows, people tend either to stay in school longer or return to school to earn new credentials. As predicted, Corinthian's enrollments grew between 2008 and 2010. As the job market stayed depressed, however, many graduates were unable to find work. As one financial analyst put it, "There were no jobs for those people to move into . . . So that creates a negative feedback loop" (Glenza, 2014). Enrollments began a downward spiral, and unemployed graduates began defaulting on their student loans at higher rates. This, in turn, brought scrutiny from regulators and began to affect Corinthian's reputation among both students and shareholders. In 2011, Corinthian reported operating losses of more than $100 million.

The U.S. Department of Education, which administers the federal student loan program, began investigating Corinthian for alleged improprieties in marketing and in required reporting about employment rates of recent graduates. The Department claimed that Corinthian was inflating employment statistics for its graduates, and engaging in other practices intended to mislead students about the value of credentials from Corinthian schools. For example, Corinthian was suspected of paying temporary employment agencies to offer "jobs" to recent graduates in order to help inflate placement rates (Lewin, 2015). In June of 2014, the Department notified Corinthian that it would be penalized by imposition of a new financial aid process that would stretch the time it took to receive federal loan payments from three days to twenty-one days. Corinthian almost immediately announced that this interruption to its cash flow cast doubt on the company's ability to survive. Unable to secure alternate financing or get relief from its creditors, Corinthian was dissolved in April of 2015. Although press stories about Corinthian's demise were filled with outcries from angry students, there was no Sweet Briar-like rally to save a beloved institution. Students were primarily concerned about obtaining debt relief for loans they had taken out to pay for programs that were now seen as worthless.

Corinthian's demise may not have been lamented by many, but defenders of for-profit higher education were outraged by what they saw as regulatory overreach by the Department of Education. Critics of the Department charged that the Obama administration was heavily biased against for-profit companies, and that unequal standards were applied to the sector in comparison with nonprofit institutions. The regulatory basis of the Department's actions against Corinthian was a set of newly devised rules requiring for-profit providers to demonstrate that its graduates were employed in reasonable numbers and at salaries sufficient to allow them to cover their student loan obligations. These "gainful employment" rules had been developed specifically for the for-profit higher education industry and did not apply to nonprofits. Critics of this policy found it unfair that an institution such as Corinthian, which was focused entirely on vocational education, should have to prove that its graduates were employable while liberal arts institutions (such as Sweet Briar), which provide few programs directly applicable to work, were not required to show that their degrees led directly to jobs.

On the other hand, other observers found in Corinthian a story that exposed what they saw as the inherent mendacity of the for-profit model. The same federal financial aid system that ultimately led to the demise of Corinthian was also the system on which its aggressive growth had been built. Federally backed student loans were first authorized in the Higher Education Act of 1965. The goal was, and remains, to assure students access to low-cost loans to enable them to study at accredited institutions of higher education. An unanticipated consequence of this policy goal has been to make large segments of the higher education industry almost entirely dependent on the availability of this form of financing. Institutions such as Corinthian relied on tuition financed by federal student loans for nearly all of their revenue. While this is also true of some not-for-profit colleges, the for-profit sector that grew rapidly in the early 2000s made the federal student loan system the explicit core of its business model. Partly fueled by the rapid growth of for-profit education, the federal government's student loan portfolio swelled to more than $1 trillion by 2016 (U.S. Department of Education, 2016).

Colleges and universities work with federally prescribed formulas to determine the amount each student can borrow. The formula takes into account the cost of attendance (including whatever tuition level the college has set), costs of living, and the students' demonstrated level of financial need. Once the student enrolls, the institution submits the loan request to the federal government and receives the funds. The institution takes its share of the proceeds (for tuition and required fees) and distributes any remainder to the student for living expenses. The system is designed to assure that the institution is paid in full before classes even meet. Thus, the cash flow of many colleges is heavily front loaded; income first, expenses later.

This system creates perverse incentives. An institution that is determined to exploit the loan program has powerful reasons to: 1) set its tuition price high so that students are forced to borrow up to the limits of their eligibility; 2) enroll as many students as possible to maximize revenue; and 3) minimize the costs of delivering services to the student. Because the institution has been paid upfront, it has little reason to worry about whether students persist in their courses or degree programs, much less whether they succeed after graduation. If the student drops out mid-semester, the institution typically is allowed to keep the revenue and the student retains the debt. From a strictly economic standpoint, a student who fails to complete a course may actually increase the institution's profit margin in the short run. A new student with fresh borrowing capacity is more valuable than one needing costly instruction and other services. Thus, the institution has incentives to invest far more in marketing and recruitment than in academic programs. Critics of for-profit higher education contend that many organizations in the sector, including Corinthian, followed this business plan to maximum effect. In Corinthian's case, the model collapsed when the government began to slow down the cash flow. The company was unable to find alternative financing sources to service its debt and operating expenses, and the risk that the Department of Education would cut off Corinthian's access to the federal loan program entirely rendered the company too risky for other investors.

Sweet Briar and Corinthian represent opposite ends of the higher education spectrum in almost every possible way, yet there are striking parallels in their stories. In both cases, the primary market signal—enrollments—turned negative. Both institutions misjudged their strengths and perhaps even misunderstood their own businesses. Colleges and universities compete for many kinds of goods, including student enrollments, philanthropic support, research grants, and ancillary revenues. They also compete for intangible assets such as reputation and goodwill. Sweet Briar apparently underestimated the value of the latter in its own case. The announcement of its closure unleashed a substantial amount of latent support that was sufficient to motivate and capitalize a fresh start. Much of this was driven by nostalgia and emotional identification (on the part of alumni), but these are highly valued features of any successful brand, and clear indicators of market strength. Sweet Briar, somewhat inadvertently, managed to monetize its brand value in a way that reduced its short-term dependance on tuition. Meanwhile, Corinthian may also be said to have misread the educational market by assuming that there would always be sufficient numbers of prospective students who were willing to take on high levels of debt for academic credentials of limited value at a time of reduced employment opportunities. When enrollments began to decline and cash flow from the federal student loan program slowed, the Corinthian model proved to be far more fragile than one might have expected of a company with more than $1 billion in annual revenue.

All educational institutions can be seen as creating both "use value" and "exchange value." Use value refers to the intrinsic benefits of the educational program: knowledge, skills, and rich experiences that contribute to a student's social and cultural capital. Exchange value refers to the potential to trade one asset for another, for instance, by using an academic credential to gain employment. In theory, these two values should be roughly equiva-lent; we should expect that the long-term intrinsic value of education should be reflected in the "purchasing power" of educational credentials for other things of value, like jobs and social standing. But these are like two curren-cies whose worth can fluctuate dramatically relative to each other. Tradi-tional residential colleges such as Sweet Briar create a high quotient of use value for their students that is at best indirectly related to employability after graduation. Benefits include knowledge and skills, but also social standing, access to influential alumni networks, and other cultural assets. These intan-gible goods become highly identified with specific college experiences that are unique to the traditions of each institution. As the Sweet Briar alumni showed, these use goods are highly prized, enough so that many were will-ing to continue paying for them through donations to the college long after their direct experiences on campus had ended. On the other hand, educa-tional providers such as Corinthian focus entirely on exchange value. The credential is a commodity, which has worth only to the extent that it leads directly to a job. When the credential declines in value—that is when the link to employment is attenuated or broken—students have buyer's remorse. They realize they have overpaid for the asset they acquired, and there is no reservoir of goodwill to sustain the relationship between the institution and its students. In sum, Sweet Briar seems to have underestimated the use value it was creating, and Corinthian overestimated the exchange value of its offerings.

A frequent critique of traditional colleges and universities is that they have become inefficient as a result of trying to do too many things. They not only provide instruction, but also operate businesses ranging from hotels (residence halls) to semiprofessional athletic teams. These wide-ranging activities require complex administrative bureaucracies and expensive facil-ities and equipment, much of which seems superfluous to the core interests of the students who pay the bills. Complexity also breeds inertia, making it difficult for institutions to react quickly to changing conditions in the environment. Thus, in recent years there have been many calls for "unbun-dling" colleges in order to streamline organizations, increase efficiency, and focus on single goals. The unbundling thesis somewhat resembles the busi-ness strategy of "no-frills" airlines, in which passengers get a seat to their destination for the price of their fare, but there are few if any amenities to make the trip more comfortable, and any extras that are available come at an additional cost. In higher education, the analogous strategy is to reduce academic services to the bare minimum necessary to allow a student to earn a credential, but to eliminate many of the services that enrich the educational experience. Although critics of this approach argue that it would exacer-bate educational disparities among students based on their ability to pay, advocates of unbundling contend that it is a necessary element of the "disruption" scenario that is often predicted for higher education. According to this view, the market can no longer tolerate the inefficiencies and ambiguous outcomes of traditional higher education, and will demand new approaches with more transparent relationships between costs and benefits.

The long history of higher education suggests that this critique is wrong, and the divergent fortunes of Sweet Briar and Corinthian offer some preliminary clues as to why this is the case. Sweet Briar, it turns out, had hidden strengths of which even its leadership was unaware. What emerged in the aftermath of the Board's closure announcement was an upwelling of support that allowed the institution to retool its programs and reconsider its strategies for the future. This hidden reservoir of goodwill was the result of the richness of experience its alumni fondly remembered, and not the result of a narrowly construed and efficiently delivered service. In contrast, Corinthian was far more vulnerable than it appeared from the outside, in part because there was no depth to its mission or programs. Corinthian's core competence, it seems in retrospect, was in originating student loans underwritten by a wary partner. Its business model was built to satisfy the requirements of that partner—the U.S. Government—not the thousands of students who were mere vehicles for transacting its business. Not surprisingly, this did not generate much goodwill when the government grew disenchanted and the institution needed both political and financial support. The surprising moral of this tale of two schools is that the would-be disrupter was disrupted, while the traditional college with its muddled mission got a second wind.

None of this is meant to suggest that educational markets will always reward the traditional institution over the non-traditional, much less the nonprofit over the commercial or the liberal arts over the vocational. There is far too great a tendency on the part of many in higher education to equate tradition with virtue, but this is an unearned assumption. A great many small colleges are in peril, and each year there are closure announcements that do not get rescinded by popular demand. Equally, there are innovative entrants in the higher education market, including for-profit companies, working with integrity on ways to improve education and broaden access to it. However, as a matter of fact, while the total number of colleges and universities in the U.S. has declined in recent years, the rate of failure has been higher within the newer, for-profit sector than among nonprofits (Lederman, 2017, July 19). Moreover, a recent study revisited the experiences of 491 "hidden colleges" (i.e., small and relatively obscure colleges, primarily residential liberal arts institutions) that were thought to be in substantial peril as long ago as the early 1970s. Researchers found that 354 (72 percent) of these institutions were still operating independently in 2017 (Tarrant, Bray, &

Katsinas, 2018). The odds of survival, even in today's rapidly changing economy, seem to continue to favor traditional institutions.

The resilience of institutions of higher education seems to defy expectations about organizational change as it applies to most corporate entities. This suggests that there are features of colleges and universities—or the higher education system more broadly—that are different from other kinds of organizations and which contribute to durability even in times of rapid external change. Identifying these features should point toward a specialized theory of organizational change in higher education.

The Higher Education Ecosystem

All organizations can be described as the interface between internal and external environments (Simon, 1969/1996). From the inside, the intentions of the leaders and members of the organization shape its purposes and ways of operating. Internal culture can be highly structured and disciplined, or it can be informal and fluid. Authority can rest with a small number of people at the top of the organization, or can be broadly distributed throughout the organization. These and other variables incorporate institutional ambitions, history, and traditions, which accumulate and modulate over time. External forces also shape organizations. These forces include market conditions (including factors such as demography), regulatory regimes, the competitive environment, and broader social demands and expectations. The unfolding history of an organization can be seen as the ongoing interplay between internal and external forces.

Human organizations can thus be regarded as parts of ecosystems, subject to many of the same evolutionary forces seen in nature. There is a "fitness" test that must be continuously met if the organization is to survive. It must be responsive to changes in the environment that are beyond its control to influence, but at the same time it must preserve the continuity and order of internal structures that sustain it. Failure to do either of these can lead to dysfunction and decline. The environment may also create the need for new kinds of organizations, either to replace older institutions that fail to respond to changing conditions, or to meet altogether new needs for which older organizations are simply not designed. The study of organizational ecology "seeks to understand how social conditions affect the rates at which new organizations and new organizational forms arise, the rates at which organizations change forms, and the rates at which organizations and forms die out" (Hannan & Freeman, 1989, p. 7). Adapting this approach for present purposes provides a more comprehensive and systemic view of higher education as an industry, albeit a loosely organized one, instead of as simply an aggregation of discrete institutions. The ecological framework exposes both how individual institutions respond to new challenges and opportunities, and how such responses shape the larger enterprise of which those institutions are a part. It is the interplay of these dynamics that moves the life stories of organizations and industries forward.

The history of American higher education offers particular opportunities to see the dynamics of organizational ecology in action (Stevens, 2015). Changes in external environments over the four hundred years since the first colleges were established in the English-speaking New World have been continuous and, at times, dramatic. Both the nation and the world have undergone political revolutions, wars, economic upheaval, demographic shifts, and technological change. Yet, a handful of institutions have survived throughout these periods of turbulence; indeed, they are among a very small number of institutions of any kind that have operated continuously since colonial times. On a shorter time-scale, social, economic, and technological changes over just the past century have been rapid and consequential, yet hundreds of colleges and universities have survived and thrived over this period of time. It is implausible to think that internal adaptations have not been required in order to keep colleges and universities in sync with changing environmental pressures. But, because the outward appearances of campus life seem so stable and uniform, it is often assumed that academia has been impervious to pressure from so-called "real world."

The longevity of colleges and universities is thus a puzzle to be solved. Furthermore, across the spectrum of American colleges and universities, one striking observation is how divergent they are with respect to size, mission, financial structure, and other variables. The fact that so many types of institutions survive simultaneously presents a second puzzle, and also a key to understanding the resilience of the entire enterprise. This is suggested by another hypothesis of the theory of organizational ecology: "A system with greater organizational diversity has a higher probability of having in hand some form that does a reasonably satisfactory job of dealing with the changed environmental conditions" (Hannan, 1989, p. 8). In nature, monocultures are often vulnerable to new environmental challenges for which they have no built-in defenses. Genetic diversity, on the other hand, preserves more potential for survivability when new defenses are called for. Organizational ecologists look for the same phenomena among institutions and industries. Higher education in the United States, for reasons perhaps unique to its history, has evolved into a loosely organized system that accommodates a broad range of institutional types. In order to understand the longevity of individual institutions and the resilience of the larger higher education enterprise, it is important to understand how and why this diverse system developed as it has. This will be the work of the next chapter.

Note

1. I owe this quip to Dr. David Korn, former dean of the Stanford School of Medicine.

Bibliography

Deresewicz, W. (2017, March 6). On political correctness: Power, class, and the new campus religion. *The American Scholar*. Retrieved from https://theamericanscholar. org/on-political-correctness/#

Donoghue, F. (2008). *The last professors: The corporate university and the fate of the humanities*. New York: Fordham University Press.

Geiger, R. (2015). *The history of American higher education: Learning and culture from the founding to World War II*. Princeton: Princeton University Press.

Glenza, J. (2014, July 28). The rise and fall of Corinthian colleges and the wake of debt it left behind. *The Guardian*. Retrieved from www.theguardian.com/education/2014/jul/28/corinthian-colleges-for-profit-education-debt-investigation

Hannan, M., & Freeman, J. (1989). *Organizational ecology*. Cambridge: Harvard University Press.

Labaree, D. (1997). Public goods, private goods: The American struggle over educational goals. *American Educational Research Journal, 34*(1), Spring, 39–81.

Labaree, D. (2017). *A perfect mess: The unlikely ascendency of American higher education*. Chicago: University of Chicago Press.

Lederman, D. (2017, April 28). Clay Christensen, doubling down. *Inside Higher Ed*. Retrieved from www.insidehighered.com/digital-learning/article/2017/04/28/clay-christensen-sticks-predictions-massive-college-closures

Lederman, D. (2017, July 19). The culling of higher ed begins. *Inside Higher Ed*. Retrieved from www.insidehighered.com/news/2017/07/19/number-colleges-and-universities-drops-sharply-amid-economic-turmoil

Lenzner, R., & Johnson, S. (1997, March 10). Seeing things as they really are. *Forbes*. Retrieved from www.forbes.com/forbes/1997/0310/5905122a.html#5ee89f1324b9

Lewin, T. (2015, April 14). Corinthian colleges fined for bogus job-placement claims. *New York Times*. Retrieved from www.nytimes.com/2015/04/15/education/corinthian-colleges-fined-for-bogus-job-placement-claims.html

Mauboussin, M., Callahan, D., & Majd, D. (2017, February 17). Corporate longevity index turnover and corporate performance. *Credit Suisse*. Retrieved from https://research-doc.credit-suisse.com/docView?language=ENG&format=PDF&sourceid=em&document_id=1070991801&serialid=TqtAPA%2FTEBUW%2BgCJnJNtlkenIBO4nHiIyPL7Muuz0FI%3D

Metzler, S. (2014). *Degrees of inequality: How the politics of higher education sabotaged the American dream*. New York: Basic Books.

O'Brien, C. (2016). Roses must be tended: The Sweet Briar College case. *Cornell Policy Review*. Retrieved from www.cornellpolicyreview.com/roses-must-be-tended-the-sweet-briar-college-case/

Selingo, J. (2013). *College (un)bound: The future of higher education and what it means for students*. Boston: Houghton Mifflin Harcourt.

Simon, H. (1969/1996). *The sciences of the artificial*. Cambridge: MIT Press.

Stevens, M. (2015). The changing ecology of US higher education. In M. Kirst & M. Stevens (Eds.), *Remaking college: The changing ecology of US higher education.* Stanford: Stanford University Press.

Sullivan, A. (2017, March 10). Is intersectionality a religion? *New York Magazine.* Retrieved from http://nymag.com/intelligencer/2017/03/is-intersectionality-a-religion.html?gtm=bottom&gtm=top

Sweet Briar College. (2017, December 15). *Sweet Briar reveals academic investments in liberal arts and sciences including core curriculum focused on leadership.* Retrieved from http://sbc.edu/news/sweet-briar-reveals-academic-investments-in-liberal-arts-and-sciences-including-core-curriculum-focused-on-leadership/

Tarrant, M., Bray, N., & Katsinas, S. (2018). The invisible colleges revisited: An empirical review. *The Journal of Higher Education, 89*(3), 341–367.

U.S. Department of Education. (2006). *A test of leadership: Charting a future of American higher education.* Washington, DC: A Report of the Commission Appointed by Secretary of Education Margaret Spellings. Retrieved from www.ed.gov/about/bdscomm/list/hiedfuture/reports/final-report.pdf

U.S. Department of Education. (2016). *Federal student aid: 2016 annual report.* Washington, DC: A Report of the Commission Appointed by Secretary of Education John King. Retrieved from https://studentaid.ed.gov/sa/sites/default/files/FY_2016_Annual_Report_508.pdf

U.S. News and World Report. (2017). *National university rankings.* Retrieved from www.usnews.com/best-colleges/rankings/national-universities?_page=3

Williams, L. (2016, September 20). How Corinthian Colleges, a for-profit behemoth, suddenly imploded. *Reveal, from the Center for Investigative Reporting.* Retrieved from www.revealnews.org/article/how-corinthian-colleges-a-for-profit-behemoth-suddenly-imploded/

3 Organizational Diversity

Colleges and universities may seem quite similar from the outside. They award similar kinds of credentials, employ similar kinds of people, are subject to common regulations, and have broadly similar traditions and conventions. But there are substantial differences among them with respect to their educational missions, their organizational and governance structures, and their financial models. Indeed, at some level it is difficult to think that a small liberal arts college, a major research university, and a community college have much in common at all, but they all offer the same nominal "product" to consumers—a higher education credential. Unlike many industries, American higher education accommodates a high degree of organizational diversity, and even considers it a distinctive strength. What is less well understood, even among many who study or work in academic organizations, is how we arrived at such variety of institutional types. As we shall see, the answer to this question reveals a great deal about how colleges and universities have responded to changing environmental conditions over the course of history.

A Time Capsule

In 1904, Homer L. Patterson, of Chicago, compiled and published the first edition of *Patterson's College and School Directory of the United States and Canada*. It was an ambitious project, claiming to be the first complete guide to all of the "schools, colleges and other institutions of higher education" (Patterson, 1904), in each state, province, and territory in North America. The Directory provides the names of superintendents of public schools for each state. Public and private institutions of higher education are listed by town or city within each state, and cross-listed by institutional type. As with any time capsule, Patterson's Directory offers both a glimpse of bygone ways of life, and the shock of familiarity as one recognizes the ties of continuity that bind us to history. It is, among other things, a useful way to explore the complicated family tree of American higher education.

Patterson counted 4,717 "institutions of higher education among the 50 states and territories of the United States in 1904."[1] This is a surprisingly large number, given that only about 2 percent of 18–24 year-olds enrolled in college around the turn of the century (U.S. Department of Education, 1993). However, the U.S. population was both growing numerically and expanding geographically. In a less mobile time, many colleges were established in order to provide local options to newly settled communities. Furthermore, the economy was being rapidly transformed by urbanization and the explosive growth of transformative new technologies. Economist Robert Gordon (2016) has argued that the century between 1870 and 1970 was the most innovative and consequential period in human history as the result of revolutions in communication (telegraphy, telephony, radio), transportation (railroads, automobiles, and air flight), and public health (antibiotics and improved sanitation systems). Patterson captures a moment at the end of the first third of this period, when a generation of interdependent institutions were forming that would foster much of this innovation and change: new cities, new industries, and new forms of higher education.

Patterson's classification scheme for institutions of higher education is not one we would use today. Table 3.1 shows the number of institutions by major category in Patterson, compared to the most commonly used current classification system developed by the Carnegie Foundation for the Advancement of Teaching.

Nearly half of the institutions on Patterson's list are preparatory schools, a term which today would refer exclusively to high schools. At the beginning of the twentieth century, the boundaries between secondary and post-secondary education were not as rigid as they seem now, however, and public high schools were not yet available in all communities. Many prep schools offered at least part of what was considered a college-level curriculum, and some even awarded bachelor's degrees. While the majority of Patterson's co-educational preparatory schools would not meet the definition of higher education today, in 1904 they offered a level of educational attainment that surpassed what was available in most public school systems—and, therefore, they were appropriately listed among institutions of higher learning.

The categories grow even less comparable to today's terminology in the lists of single-sex schools. "Preparatory colleges for women" includes, again, many institutions that today would be considered little more than private high schools. But this category also captures colleges such as Bryn Mawr, Vassar, and Wellesley, which were founded as full equivalents to all-male colleges and universities, as well as dozens of other academies, seminaries, and institutes that provided parallel, if unequal, opportunities

Table 3.1 Classification Systems of U.S. Institutions of Higher Education

Patterson's Directory, 1904		Carnegie Classifications, 2018	
Universities and Colleges	504	Doctoral Universities	335
Preparatory Schools—Co-Educational	1430	Master's Colleges and Universities	741
Military and Boys Prep	388	Baccalaureate Colleges	583
Colleges for Women and Girls Prep	724	Baccalaureate/Associates	408
Normal Schools	305	Associate's Colleges	1113
Agricultural, Industrial, Mining, and Technical	123	Special Focus 2 Year	444
Law Schools	106	Special Focus 4 Year	1005
Medical Schools—Regular	138	Tribal Colleges	35
Medical Schools—Homeopathic	19	Total	4664
Medical Schools—Eclectic	9		
Medical Schools—Physio-Medical	2		
Medical Schools—Postgraduate	3		
Schools of Osteopathy	5		
Schools of Dentistry	55		
Schools of Pharmacy	59		
Veterinary Schools	12		
Schools of Theology	22		
Schools of Music	54		
Art Schools	77		
Elocution, Oratory, and Dramatic Art	24		
Business, Shorthand, and Telegraphy	627		
Miscellaneous Schools	31		
Total	4717		

for women. Similarly, Patterson's list of schools and military academies for boys includes notable entries such as West Point, which was not only a training ground for army officers, but also the nation's first college of engineering.

As a jarring reminder of a history that still has pernicious effects on higher education today, Patterson lists institutions segregated by race within many categories, revealing another parallel but unequal system. If the name of the institution is not sufficiently obvious as to its segregated purpose (e.g. The State Normal School for Colored Students, in Montgomery, Alabama), Patterson makes it clear in the brief description for each entry.

Despite the differences in taxonomy between Patterson and Carnegie, there are lines of continuity. Among the 504 "Universities and Colleges" in Patterson's list—institutions most clearly similar to today's academic organizations—there are public universities in every state, along with many leading private institutions still operating today. By 1904, most of today's prominent colleges and universities were already well established, and the roster of names is readily familiar.

Reading Patterson today also reminds us that higher education has long had its marginal players, ranging from entrepreneurs responding to new market opportunities to more fringe elements selling educational snake oil. The Directory lists 627 "business schools," for example. Although business schools began appearing on university campuses as early as 1881, with the founding of the Wharton School at the University of Pennsylvania, most business education amounted to training in entry-level skills such as book-keeping, stenography, and shorthand. Patterson grouped these schools—many of which were proprietary regional franchises—with schools for training telegraph operators. If, as it is sometimes said, the telegraph was the first internet, schools of telegraphy were the equivalents of today's coding boot camps. Then, as now, they provided students with the minimal training necessary for entry-level technical positions to serve a fast-growing new industry.

In 1904 schools of art, music, and other creative endeavors also sat on the edges of higher education. The Kelso School of Music and Dramatic Art in Chicago, and the Lawrence School of Acting in New York represent the type. Then, as now, such schools of art catered to the hope of many students, however realistic, that their artistic passions would sustain them economically.

Patterson also reminds us that professional schools in fields such as medicine and law originated primarily outside of colleges and universities, but within a broader concept of higher education. Their training programs were a mix of classroom didactics and apprenticeship, but they were seldom grounded in research. These programs were not considered to be postgraduate (i.e., restricted to those with a bachelor's degree) until the early twentieth century. Training in medicine would not begin to take its modern form until after Abraham Flexner published a scathing critique of the state of medical education in 1910. Only then did many universities take up the work of training physicians as a genuine academic pursuit, and as a result, the era of independent medical colleges largely came to an end, along with much of the experimentation in "eclectic" and other alternative theories of medicine that comprise separate categories in Patterson's list. Similarly, law schools became associated with universities as part of the legal profession's strategy to upgrade itself and require more standardized and rigorous training than one might receive by merely "reading for the law" under the supervision of a practicing attorney, as was typical in earlier times.

In summary, Patterson's snapshot of higher education in 1904 shows more than a passing family resemblance to the industry today—although it is a sepia-toned image from a very different time. Most of the current major organizational forms are found, at least in their early stages. There are large universities and small colleges, public, and private institutions, nonprofit and for-profit schools, mainstream, and experimental institutions, those devoted to vocational training and those offering classical liberal arts, and so forth. There are even correspondence schools, which serve as the precursors to today's internet-based distance learning institutions. The lineage from 1904 to today is not difficult to trace, in part because many of the institutions from Patterson's time still exist today. Of the 504 "colleges and universities" listed by Patterson, 82 percent of them are still operating. At the same time, we see a large and colorful group of more marginal institutions that arose to serve specialized interests and to capitalize on moments of opportunity. While many fewer individual institutions in these fringe categories continue to exist, the phenomenon of experimentation and novelty continues. There is strong evidence, then, for both change and continuity from 1904 until the present.

Accretive Change

Like all time capsules, Patterson's Directory preserves a specific moment, but we are left to wonder what previous dynamics led to such a diverse configuration of institutions. In the broadest sense, the diversity of organizational types in America is a byproduct of the lack of centralized authority over higher education. In most countries, colleges and universities were, and to some extent remain, creatures of either the state or the church. The U.S. is unusual in the extent to which higher education has developed without strong national or ecclesiastical policies about what kinds of institutions can offer educational programs, or what those programs should entail. Even when the government has taken an active role in education, it has done so primarily through indirect incentives rather than strict mandates. In the absence of a strong prescriptive regime, U.S. higher education has spawned several distinct organizational types, each of which represents a response to particular environmental signals. Individual institutions have been free to improvise their own responses to these signals; nevertheless, strong patterns have emerged with each cycle of major change. By tracing the influence of three specific external dynamics on institutional formation, we begin to see the outlines of a theory of change for higher education—one that I shall call "accretive change."

The story of higher education's evolution and adaptation to changing times can be seen as a series of responses to these three factors:

1. The emergence of a new social purpose or mission for higher education;
2. New organizational models that are adapted to the purposes of higher education;
3. New sources of capital to finance innovation.

What remains unusual about higher education compared to many other industries is that the resulting new institutional forms often take their place alongside older forms, thus adding to the diversity of the overall enterprise. In this respect, change comes to higher education as a matter of accretion rather than disruption.

A Brief History of Change

The time period spanning the founding of Harvard in 1636 through the Civil War is important for a full understanding of the history of American higher education, but it serves mainly as stage setting for present purposes. We might characterize this period as a time of market formation, in which a baseline set of competitors was being assembled. Given the nation's rapid westward expansion, especially after the Revolutionary War, colleges were founded at an unprecedented rate in order to serve new settlements. To the extent that there was competition, it was among the various religious denominations for which the founding of a college was a way to spread their particular version of moral virtue, which was often closely associated with higher learning. I often use my own hometown and alma mater as examples of this period of institution building. Galesburg, Illinois, was founded in 1837 by a Congregationalist community from upstate New York (Calkins, 1937/1989). Their first two acts of settlement on the open prairie were to erect a church on the town square, and to found Knox College a short distance away. These were the two cultural institutions around which the town would quickly develop. By the time of Patterson's Directory, less than seventy years later, Galesburg had a population of 18,000 and was the center of a thriving local economy built on agriculture and the railroads. By then it also had a second college, established by Universalists, called Lombard College. Within a circumference of 60 miles from Galesburg there were also colleges founded by Methodists, Presbyterians, Lutherans, and Catholics, in addition to a proprietary school of business (part of a chain of schools operating around the state), a secular private college, and two normal schools for training teachers.

This pattern of growth, typical of many emerging communities in the Midwest, led to something of an arms race and an oversupply of higher education options in some areas, but differentiation was slight beyond the style of chapel services required. Most denominational colleges offered essentially the same liberal arts curriculum with its heavy emphasis on classical literature, math, and rudimentary science. For the most part, these were exceedingly small institutions by today's standards. Labaree (2017) cites evidence that the average college enrolled fewer than fifty students by 1850. These institutions were also financially precarious. Very few had capital resources beyond some illiquid assets in the form of land and a few buildings, and cash income from tuition was meager. Of those five denominational colleges in and around my hometown in 1904, two closed their doors not long after making their appearance in Patterson's Directory. The proprietary business college and one of the normal schools are also gone; the other normal school was absorbed into the state university system. As the contours of development in newly settled areas became better defined, the emerging higher education industry began to sort itself out in response to local and national market demands.

Of all of the institutional types represented in and around Galesburg, the liberal arts college represents the most durable form, even though the attrition rate among them was high. Loosely modeled on the collegiate system contained within English universities, they focused on subjects that represented high culture and refinement, including classics, the arts, history, and science (Thelin, 2004). These disciplines were often personified by just a few faculty members, they required little in the way of infrastructure to teach them, and there were no regulatory requirements to meet. Thus, the "barriers to entry" for establishing new colleges were low and inexpensive. What is less obvious is where the motivation came from to start these colleges on the edges of civilization. In the context of the American frontier, the proliferation of colleges can be seen as a somewhat desperate attempt to retain ties to an increasingly distant European cultural heritage. To the extent that pioneering societies continued to hold this heritage in high regard even amid the challenges of settling a wild, new continent, the liberal arts college movement served an important civilizing purpose.

Liberal arts colleges thus can be seen as the original model of American higher education. They were themselves local adaptations of a higher education tradition inherited from Europe, with novel forms of financing and governance, but modified to meet the needs and constraints of an emerging local culture. For our purposes they form the baseline from which to measure subsequent change.

The Land-Grant Movement

Against this backdrop of grass roots market formation in the first half of the nineteenth century, interventions of the federal government constituted the first great potentially disruptive force in American higher education. The Morrill Act of 1862, also known as the Land-Grant Act, represented an ambitious new public commitment to higher education, undertaken as one of several initiatives meant to accelerate the westward settlement of the continent and provide an adequately skilled labor force for the rapidly developing economy.

The three factors that drive accretive change in higher education are apparent in the emergence of land-grant universities. First, they represented a new public purpose for higher education, and therefore a new educational mission. The land-grant colleges were closely associated with interest in "practical arts," a neologism of the time intended to complement, if not contrast with, the traditional liberal arts. These new institutions "were predicated on the equivalence of agriculture, mechanic arts, and other professional studies with the liberal arts." (Geiger, 2015, p. 288). Venturing into these fields within the framework of the university represented a significant departure from prevailing classically oriented theories of education, which held that practical skills were inferior to higher intellectual pursuits.

This new academic mission led to a second feature of accretive change. The new practical arts disciplines introduced organizational complexity to the institutions that housed them. The older liberal arts colleges scarcely needed much internal organization since all of the faculty were jointly involved in a common and non-technical curriculum—often under the tight control of a dominant president and local board of trustees. Diversity and specialization gave rise to sharper boundaries within the faculty, the first step toward multi-school universities, as well as new layers of middle managers such as deans and vice presidents. The new land-grant universities were also intended and designed for scale in a way that none of the older colleges were. Cornell, one of the beneficiaries of New York State's land grant, had an inaugural entering class of 412 students in 1868, (Geiger, 2015, p. 289), eight times larger than the entire four-year enrollment of the average college of that period. The University of Michigan, which had its origins in an earlier territorial college, grew from seven students in 1841 to more than 1,200 in 1865 (Peckham, 1967). Since they were built to serve new states and territories in their entirety, the land-grant universities introduced growth and expansion as central strategic goals.

The third necessary element in the theory of accretive change is the appearance of a new form of capital to finance innovation. The Land-Grant Act provides a strong example: In the first Morrill Act of 1862, Congress allocated to the states some 17,430 acres of public land which could be sold or directly used to found new public universities (Rudolph, 1962). Land values varied widely from state to state, and the disposition of some land was clearly mishandled through incompetence and fraud, but sales resulted in an average price of $1.65 per acre (ibid.). This resulted in an infusion of some $28.8 Million (in 1860 dollars) in new capital in support of higher education in the United States. The equivalent value in 2017 would be more than $800 million. Given the impecunious position of most established colleges at the time, this investment represented an unprecedented infusion of wealth into what became a national higher education project.

Land-grant universities served as regional magnets for aspiring students, many of whom might not have been interested in the liberal arts, nor would they likely have been regarded as "college material" at more traditional institutions. They also opened enrollment to women as full participants in the university. Public universities, which continue to serve the vast majority of students in the U.S. today, represented an important step toward democratizing higher education. In many ways, they supplanted the older liberal arts institutions as the "standard model" for U.S. higher education, at least in terms of enrollments. Yet, while they also represented new competition for older institutions, public land-grant universities did not fully displace older models. During a time of rapid population growth, and with broader segments of the population participating, the overall market for higher education expanded dramatically, creating opportunities for new institutions and many older ones, alike. While many smaller colleges succumbed to declining enrollments in the latter half of the nineteenth century, the basic form of the liberal arts college persisted and even thrived alongside new public universities.

Doctoral Universities

Another educational concern arose roughly in parallel to the practical arts movement in the mid-1800s. A group of emerging and highly ambitious academic leaders became interested in graduate education, and specifically in the German university models, which were then regarded as the best in the world. The founding presidents of Johns Hopkins, the University of Chicago, and Stanford are often cited as the leading emissaries of this new vision of American higher education. Daniel Coit Gilman, William Rainey Harper, and David Starr Jordan, respectively, founded their new "start-up" institutions with explicit goals to beat the Germans at their own game. In doing so, they re-envisioned the structure and functions of the American university once again.

The blueprints for these universities varied from one to the next, but they all began from the premise that research and teaching are mutually reinforcing functions—and that graduate student training, in particular, should be grounded in the discovery of new knowledge. Shortly after the establishment of Johns Hopkins, Gilman explained the strategic vision that motivated him and his Board of Trustees: ". . . there seemed to be a demand for scientific laboratories and professorships, the directors of which should be free to pursue their own researches, stimulating their students to prosecute study with a truly scientific spirit and aim. " (Cole, 2009, p. 19). It is difficult from our current perspective to appreciate how much of a departure this was from extant educational philosophy. In contrast, for example, John Cardinal Newman, perhaps the most influential academician in the English-speaking world at the time, had argued that the purpose of the university was to create time and space for students to develop philosophical and theological habits of mind (Newman, 1852/1999). His treatise scarcely recognizes the importance of original investigation, experimentation, or the search for new knowledge. The rising American leaders of higher education rejected Newman's "idea of a university" almost entirely.

Thus, in what is now beginning to look like a pattern, a group of upstart institutions launched themselves upon the world with a new educational purpose and important new approaches to institution building and governance. They had important effects on the larger higher education enterprise, far beyond the boundaries of their own campuses. For one thing, they created a new kind of free-agency market for academic stars. Harper was especially aggressive in his search for talent to populate the new University of Chicago, persuading several sitting college presidents to join his new faculty by opening day, (Boyer, 2015) along with leading scholars across several fields, among them Albert Michelson, who would soon become the first American Nobel laureate. With so many ambitious institutions forming at roughly the same time, an unprecedented demand for academic talent developed. This sellers' market for faculty brought new institutional power to the professoriate. As one historian of Columbia University observed, during the late nineteenth century, faculty rose to a position of "effective parity" with the Board of Trustees, whose role in governance had been absolute in earlier generations (McCaughey, 2003). The origin of the first national professional association of faculty is often traced to a dispute over academic freedom that occurred at Stanford in 1901, which pitted a faculty member against the surviving founder of the University, Jane Stanford, and her allies on the Board of Trustees (American Association of University Professors, n.d.). Although in this case the faculty member lost his job, the very idea that a lowly professor could challenge the powerful patroness of the university marked a turning point in the political structure of institutions. Shared governance—the idea that administration and faculty have separate spheres of control within the institution, was a remarkable organizational innovation that, to this day, is an adaptation unique to higher education.

As with the land-grant universities, the new research universities depended on new sources of capital to finance their ambitious goals. A new era might be said to have begun with Johns Hopkins' gift of $7 million to the institution that would soon bear his name (Gilman, 1876). Considering that Harvard's then-260 year-old endowment was no more than $12 million (Cole, 2009, p. 34), it is clear that the new institution began with a more than respectable asset base. In current dollars, Hopkins' founding gift would be worth on the order of $200 million. John D. Rockefeller financed Harper's aggressive spending to the tune of $5 million initially, which was fully matched by other donors and frequently supplemented by Rockefeller and others during the university's early years (Boyer, 2015). Many other industrialists of the Gilded Age (Vanderbilt, Carnegie, Rice, Stanford) became the founders or benefactors of universities at previously unprecedented levels. By 1900, annual revenues for higher education from both gifts and "productive funds" (i.e., endowment investments) had roughly doubled from annual levels during the previous decade, totaling $17 million, or nearly $500 million in current dollars (Sears, 1922, p. 55). Thus, "universities for the first time had a permanent financial base" (Thelin, 2004, p. 127). The new institutions, and older ones revived by new levels of philanthropy, ceased living hand to mouth and were able to plan for more ambitious and sustainable futures.

The ambitions of the new doctoral universities presented a clear challenge to prestigious, older institutions, including those whose origins dated back to colonial times. Some members of the old guard reasserted their traditional liberal arts, and primarily undergraduate, missions. Others began to remodel themselves and adopt some of the practices emerging at the start-ups. Yale's history during this period is illustrative: The period from 1871 to 1886 has been called a time of "stagnation" by one historian of Yale (Kelley, 1974) because of the failure of university leaders to move with the times. With the ascendance of the new doctoral university model, the leaders of Yale were conflicted about whether to remain committed to their undergraduate, liberal arts, and religious legacies or embrace modernity. During a presidential transition in 1870, various competing voices emerged. Timothy Dwight V. lobbied the trustees to embrace the new model, estimating that it would require new investments of $3.5 million to achieve. At the time, Yale's permanent funds totaled just $1 million. Dwight's proposal was considered too great a financial reach, and conservative sentiments prevailed for financial, academic, and religious reasons. A more traditional president was selected. It was not until Dwight became president himself in 1886 that he was in a position to begin instituting his vision. He convinced the Board to change the name of the institution to Yale University (from Yale College), reorganized the schools and appointed ambitious new deans, and began expanding enrollments. He also began raising funds at a rate that was previously unprecedented at Yale, such that by 1899 the permanent assets of the university rose to $4.5 million, (Kelley, 1974, p. 276) thus closing the $3.5 million funding gap he had foreseen nearly thirty years earlier. Yale joined the flagship colonial colleges of Harvard, Princeton, Columbia, and the University of Pennsylvania as converts to the new doctoral university model, all of which thereby renewed their leases at the top of the American academic hierarchy.

Community Colleges

The doctoral university model that ultimately became standardized in the United States was something of a compromise. Older universities like Harvard built a graduate and research superstructure on the foundations of their undergraduate colleges. The new startup institutions generally adopted this same model, although some purists felt that non-specialized undergraduate education did not belong in a place devoted to advanced research. Chicago's Harper was perhaps the most consumed by this among the generation of founding presidents, and he entertained a number of potential solutions (Boyer, 2015). One proposal was to eliminate the first two years of college and accept students only after they were prepared to pursue specialized studies. Another proposal under consideration for a time was to establish a separate but adjacent "junior college" that would specialize in general education and serve as a feeder to the university.

Although he abandoned this plan within the structure of the University of Chicago itself, Harper was instrumental in founding the first junior college in nearby Joliet, Illinois, in 1901 (Drury, 2003). It was based at a local high school, and was intended to prepare students for entry to Chicago or another university after roughly two years of general study. The legacy of this college-preparation model remains a core purpose of many community colleges today.

The junior college idea quickly became the answer to a variety of additional educational problems. At a time of rapid industrialization and urbanization, employers demanded more skilled workers than could be produced by the university system, even operating at its new, larger scale. Employers also needed very specific skills that did not require a university degree, such as bookkeeping and stenography, as well as skilled trades. Furthermore, since many land-grant institutions had been constructed away from urban centers in order to have space to grow and to serve rural communities, access became increasingly problematic for workers in cities. As business and industry became increasingly concentrated in city centers, junior colleges arose to serve growing populations of urban dwellers. As American cities also became more ethnically diverse, community colleges began to serve as centers for acculturation for immigrants, often providing English language and citizenship instruction along with vocational training and college preparation.

Junior colleges once again illustrate the model of accretive change. They were created to fill a new educational niche (or rather, multiple educational niches) and thus arose with a mission that is distinct from both liberal arts colleges and universities. They clearly represented a new institutional type: non-residential, often adult-oriented, and governed by local community boards. The third element of the change model also soon appeared when states and municipalities began to support community colleges with local tax revenues. California led the way with a series of legislative actions between 1907 and 1917 that established independent junior college districts with the power to levy local taxes (Drury, 2003). Although public universities also received tax-payer support, they did so as part of the general appropriations process at the state level, and in competition with other state budget priorities. Community colleges were similar to K-12 school districts with the ability to make much more focused and local claims on public support (Tollefson, 2009).

The National R&D System and Massification

A fourth example of institutional change came after World War II, when public demands on universities once again changed substantially. The war had been won in part on the strength of American technology, and its final acts in Hiroshima and Nagasaki were stunning, though horrific, examples of the power of organized "big science" and applied research. To achieve that result, the U.S. government had created a sophisticated network comprising universities, the military, and federally employed scientists, the collective power of which greatly amplified the scope and impact of research that could be accomplished at any single institution. After the war, Vanever Bush, the Director of the federal Office of Scientific Research and Development, recommended that it was in the nation's interest to maintain this R&D network, with universities at its major nodes (Bush, 1945). Thus began a new mission for doctoral universities that soon had substantial organizational and financial consequences.

The modern alliance between federal research priorities and university research agendas did not come without controversy, especially in the 1960s when student protests over military research boiled up into violence on some campuses. The system quickly became entrenched, however, and led to elaborate new organizational structures for the management and governance of large-scale research. University administrative offices grew and became far more professionalized. Many faculty members became contractors of the government, albeit through elaborate institutional structures, with incentives not only to pursue basic research but to manage the emerging intellectual property with an eye toward commercialization. Stanford was perhaps the most aggressive university in making the new research regime the centerpiece of its strategic plan. Fred Terman, Stanford's provost during the 1950s, seized the opportunity to build new "steeples of excellence" in research—which, he correctly foresaw, would greatly enhance the university's financial strength by bringing in support for faculty, students, staff, and facilities (Lowen, 1997). Decisions about which faculty to recruit and which departments to build were based not only on academic priorities, but also on their potential to attract federal research dollars.

Concurrent with the new research and development regime, the federal government provided another form of stimulus to higher education in the form of the GI Bill. World War II had disrupted a generation of potential students, and policy makers wanted to give them opportunities to fully participate in the quickly modernizing economy. The GI Bill provided educational benefits to some nine million Americans, greatly expanding the college-going population and further normalizing higher education as a middle-class ambition. Thus, while many of the elite universities focused on building their research portfolios, other institutions undertook dramatic expansions of enrollment, which in turn led to growth in faculty and staff numbers, as well as facilities. Collectively, this period of "massification" (Gumport, Iannozzi, Shaman, & Zemsky, 1997) marked the largest increase in the capacity of the U.S. higher education system in its history.

Thus, two somewhat different variations on the basic university type emerged in the postwar era, each of which is a response to changes in the environment. Research universities became highly selective in their faculty hires and student admissions, and they worked to optimize their opportunities to attract financial support, not only from the federal government but also from foundations and private donors. A next tier of institutions pursued a more open and expansive focus on teaching, built on both popular demand for access and public policy that encouraged it. The emerging division of labor between doctoral research pursuits and mass education was made most explicit in Clark Kerr's 1960 Master Plan for Higher Education in California, which for the first time among the states denoted clear differences in purpose between University of California and California State University campuses, and in the students they were meant to serve (Kerr, 1960).

The twin stimuli of federal research programs and expanded financial aid tended to transform existing institutions rather than stimulate the creation of new ones; the postwar years represent another distinct phase of accretive change. Enormous new resources flowed into existing institutions, designed to incentivize new activities. Institutions responded with vigor, embarking on ambitious new strategic plans and missions. This, in turn, produced profound changes in their organizational structures and cultures. Research universities became, in effect, large scale federal contractors, and they learned to become adept at managing within complex, highly regulated financial and legal environments. Their administrative structures came to resemble those of other large corporations, dominated by lawyers and financial officers who brought new management disciplines to the oversight of academic organizations. In parallel, other institutions grew enrollments at unprecedented levels, adding student services and amenities that required entirely new management specialties, from financial aid administration to student counseling. Universities of both types became more dominated by the kinds of management cultures that existed in other enterprises, complete with complex organizational hierarchies, highly paid professional administrators, and burgeoning ranks of specialized workers. Much to the dismay of many faculty members, politicians, and tuition-paying families, administrative costs in both variants of the modern university began to exceed the amounts spent on instruction and direct academic services, and grew at much faster rates from year to year (Snyder & Galambos, 1988).

Online, For-Profit

The most recent wave of change in higher education represents the confluence of several new developments that began to appear in the late 1990s. These developments include the rise of the internet as a new way to deliver courses at massive scale, together with the emergence of investors hungry for the next new thing in technology. Higher education was seen by many as a "killer app," which would dwarf other emerging uses of technology (Forbes Magazine, 2000).

Among the organizations to capitalize on these trends, the University of Phoenix was the most prominent, and it came to symbolize the new industry of for-profit, distance education providers. It must be noted that neither for-profit education, nor "distance learning," were new inventions. Proprietary colleges have existed since colonial times, and correspondence programs have been available for a century (Rudolph, 1962/1990). What was truly new about the University of Phoenix and its imitators was the scale of their ambitions. By 2010, enrollments at Phoenix peaked more than 470,000 (McKenzie, 2018). From 2000 to 2010, undergraduate enrollments at for-profit institutions grew by 329 percent, to a total of some 1.7 million students (U.S. Department of Education, 2018).

The explosion of growth in online education followed the same pattern as many other internet-driven industries, with new forms of venture capital being an important common denominator. Unlike traditional lenders, "VCs," as venture capitalists are known, make large investments unsecured by hard assets, in exchange for substantial equity stakes in new companies. Such high-risk investments demand the potential of extraordinarily high rewards, which almost invariably can only be achieved through massive growth. Thus, the capacity for online education to serve large numbers of students at relatively low marginal cost is an ideal business model for financiers concerned primarily with growth. These factors, combined with the availability of federal student loan programs to underwrite student enrollments, made online education and related educational technologies powerful magnets for venture capital. In the first six months of 2015 alone, more than $2.5 billion was invested in educational technology and services, (ICEF Monitor, 2015) and the scale of investment has remained high for more than a decade.

Along with new technology and new financing methods, the new online universities benefited from a third important trend. Rapid shifts in employment patterns created pressure on employed adults to acquire new skills. Many working adults who had either only a high school degree or an incomplete college degree found themselves at a great disadvantage in the work force. They often found traditional colleges and universities inaccessible since their programs were primarily offered during the day, for full-time students. Some adults were also reluctant to reenter college life dominated, as it was, by the culture of late adolescence. Online learning offered convenience, flexibility, and a degree of anonymity to an entirely new market of students who were otherwise poorly served by traditional institutions. Perhaps the most important innovation introduced by online institutions was their ability to accommodate new students almost immediately by dispensing with the traditional academic calendar. Courses begin weekly, turning education nearly into an impulse purchase, rather than a life-changing decision for which one might have to prepare for a year or more.

The new online universities represent a dramatically different organizational structure compared to traditional institutions. As we shall discuss in more detail in the next chapter, the typical online institution nearly eliminates full-time faculty and thereby spends less than half of the amount that traditional institutions devote to instruction costs, as a percentage of budget. This remodeling of the instructional workforce creates room for substantially larger expenditures on marketing and technology, as well as higher salaries for senior managers and, critically, profits to distribute back to investors. The balance of power between faculty and administrators that has been honored (if not always observed) in traditional institutions is largely dispensed with in for-profit models, and research is non-existent. The new online institutions eliminate many university services (student activities, advising, athletics) and capital expenses for campus facilities. Furthermore, they typically focus on academic programs that are directly related to career preparation, with little attention paid to electives that other institutions regard as important to a well-rounded, liberal education.

Critics argue that these departures from the traditional academic model result in inferior, if not inadequate, educational programs. Defenders of the new model, on the other hand, regard the streamlining of services as a way of promoting efficiency and access, and eliminating waste for students whose goals are primarily instrumental.

For present purposes, we need only note that the large for-profit institutions that emerged in the early years of the new millennium once again fit the pattern of earlier waves of accretive change. Generally, they were established to serve a new variation on higher education's mission, they adopted new organizational structures to serve that mission, and they were created with new sources of capital, in this case the private equity or venture capital markets.

The Persistence of Diversity

Table 3.2 displays the characteristics of change that have been briefly described in the foregoing paragraphs. My argument so far has been that these waves of organizational innovation occur in response to three kinds of environmental stimuli. Interestingly, however, these new forms of organization do not tend to push aside earlier forms. Higher education tends to absorb new institutional types into the collective enterprise, thus adding to diversity across the industry.

Table 3.2 Characteristics of Change in Higher Education

Institutional Type	Mission	Organizational Innovation	Source of Capital
Liberal arts colleges	Liberal arts	Small residential community	Tuition, church, and community support
Land-grant universities	Practical arts	Large-scale, multi-School	Federal transfer of assets to states
Doctoral universities	Doctoral education	Shared governance for faculty	Private philanthropy
Community colleges	General education and job skills	Community based, open Access	Local tax authority
R&D universities, massification	Federal R&D contractors, college as a middle-class expectation	Large-scale research administration, vast student services	Federal R&D budget, federal student grant and loan programs
For-profit, online universities	Working adults	Corporate, minimal faculty governance	Venture capital

To illustrate this phenomenon, let us draw from one additional example from higher education's history. In January of 1900, a joint letter from five university presidents went out to a select group of colleagues inviting them to a meeting in Chicago the following month (Association of American Universities, n.d.). The fourteen institutions represented at the meeting were the most prominent doctoral-granting universities in the country, and their reason for gathering was, essentially, to engage in a joint effort at brand building. American doctoral programs were still, at that time, seen as inferior to those offered by European universities, especially those in Germany. The university leaders who gathered in Chicago in February of 1900 were determined to make American doctoral programs fully competitive on a global level—and to build a homegrown generation of American scholars who could command respect around the world. Thus, the founding presidents of what would become the Association of American Universities (AAU) gathered as a kind of trade group, with the goal of enhancing their individual reputations by promoting the collective brand.

The founding AAU members came from all three of the institutional types extant in America at that time: Harvard, Yale, Columbia, Princeton, and Pennsylvania had been founded as liberal arts colleges in the Colonial era. Cornell and the Universities of Michigan, Wisconsin, and California were leaders among the new land-grant institutions. Johns Hopkins, Chicago, Stanford, Clark, and the Catholic University of America were among the generation of doctoral universities founded through private philanthropy in the late nineteenth century. What seems extraordinary in retrospect is that none of them sought predominance either for their own institutions or for their "type." Each of them might have laid claim to representing the best approach to doctoral education. The old line colonial schools had the benefit of long, distinguished pedigrees and the preeminence of their reputations. The new private universities had unprecedented support from the reigning titans of American industry; the innovators who had delivered the industrial revolution to the country and, in the process, refashioned life itself. The public universities represented the most visible expression of commitment from both federal and state governments to the urgent importance of higher education, and they were therefore monuments to the will of the people and manifestations of higher education as a democratic ambition. It was the perfect opportunity for one segment or the other to attempt to push its competitors aside and claim the future for itself. In fact, however, there was recognition that all of these institutional forms were functionally equal and all added value in promoting an emerging collective reputation. Few other industries could be expected to exhibit such a high degree of ecumenicism.

Today's higher education landscape includes examples of each of the institutional types we have discussed. The collective enterprise tends to preserve and multiply a diversity of forms rather than reduce itself to a single new model. As the theory of organizational ecology predicts, this diversity provides resilience to the industry as a whole because it offers a variety of responses to new environmental challenges. The theory of accretive change that I have proposed suggests that higher education implicitly recognizes this and accepts innovative forms into its fold relatively easily. In the next chapter, we shall explore this thesis in greater detail, especially as it relates to the idea of disruption.

Note

1. This includes what we now refer to as the lower forty-eight states plus the District of Columbia and Indian Territory.

Bibliography

American Association of University Professors. (n.d.). Retrieved from www.aaup. org/about/history-aaup

Association of American Universities. (n.d.). *The letter of invitation to the founding conference of AAU*. Retrieved from www.aau.edu/sites/default/files/AAUFiles/ KeyIssues/Budgets%26Appropriations/FY17/Invit.pdf

Boyer, J. (2015). *The University of Chicago: A history*. Chicago: University of Chicago Press.

Bush, V. (1945). *Science, the endless frontier*. Retrieved from www.nsf.gov/od/lpa/ nsf50/vbush1945.htm

Calkins, E. E. (1937/1989). *They broke the prairie: Being some account of the settlement of the upper Mississippi valley by religious and educational pioneers, told in terms of one city, Galesburg, and of one college Knox*. Galesburg, IL: Knox College.

The Carnegie Classification of Institutions of Higher Education. (n.d.). *About carnegie classification*. Retrieved from http://carnegieclassifications.iu.edu/

Cole, J. R. (2009). *The great American university: Its rise to preeminence, its indispensable national role, why it must be protected*. New York: Public Affairs, a Member of the Perseus Group.

Drury, R. (2003). Community colleges in America: A historical perspective. *Inquiry*, *8*(1). Retrieved from https://files.eric.ed.gov/fulltext/EJ876835.pdf

Forbes Magazine. (2000). *The virtual classroom vs. the real one*. Retrieved from https://forbes.com/bow/2000/0911/bestofweb_print.html

Geiger, R. (2015). *The history of American higher education: Learning and culture from the founding to World War II*. Princeton: Princeton University Press.

Gilman, D. (1876). *Inaugural address*. Retrieved from www.jhu.edu/about/history/ gilman-address

Gordon, R. J. (2016). *The rise and fall of American growth: The U.S. standard of living since the Civil War*. Princeton: Princeton University Press.

Gumport, P., Iannozzi, M., Shaman, S., & Zemsky, R. (1997). *Trends in United States higher education from massification to post-massification*. National Center for

Postsecondary *Improvement, Stanford University*. Retrieved from https://web.stanford.edu/group/ncpi/documents/pdfs/1-04_massification.pdf

ICEF Monitor (2015). *Investments in education technology reaching new heights in 2015*. Retrieved from Monitor.icef.com/2015/08/investments-in-education-technology-reaching-new-heights-in-2015/

Kelley, B. M. (1974). *Yale: A history*. New Haven: Yale University Press.

Kerr, C. (1960). *A master plan for higher education in California, 1960–1975*. Sacramento: A Report of the California State Department of Education. Retrieved from www.lib.berkeley.edu/uchistory/archives_exhibits/masterplan/MasterPlan1960.pdf

Labaree, D. (2017). *A perfect mess: The unlikely ascendency of American higher education*. Chicago: University of Chicago Press.

Lowen, R. (1997). *Creating the cold war university: The transformation of Stanford*. Berkeley: University of California Press.

McCaughey, R. (2003). *Stand, Columbia: A history of Columbia University in the city of New York, 1754–2004*. New York: Columbia University Press.

McKenzie, L. (2018, April 23). The 100K club. *Inside Higher Ed*. Retrieved from www.insidehighered.com/news/2018/04/23/nonprofits-poised-unseat-u-phoenix-largest-online-university

Newman, J. (1852/1999). *The idea of a university*. Washington, DC: Regnery.

Patterson, H. (1904). *Patterson's college and school directory of the United States and Canada*. Chicago: American Educational Co.

Peckham, H. (1967). *The making of the University of Michigan*. Ann Arbor: University of Michigan Press.

Rudolph, F. (1962/1990). *The American college and university: A history*. Athens: University of Georgia Press.

Sears, J. B. (1922/1990). *Philanthropy in the history of American higher education*. Brunswick: Transaction Publishers.

Snyder, T., & Galambos, E. (1988). *Administrative costs: Continuing the study*. Washington, DC: US Department of Education, Office of Educational Research and Improvement.

Thelin, J. R. (2004). *A history of American higher education*. Baltimore: Johns Hopkins University Press.

Tollefson, T. A. (2009). Community college governance, funding, and accountability: A century of issues and trends. *Community College Journal of Research and Practice, 33*(3–4), 386–402.

U.S. Department of Education. (1993). *120 years of American education: A statistical portrait*. Washington, DC: A Report of the National Center for Education Statistics Appointed by Secretary of Education Lamar Alexander. Retrieved from https://nces.ed.gov/pubs93/93442.pdf

U.S. Department of Education. (2018). *The condition of education*. National Center for Education Statistics. Retrieved from https://nces.ed.gov/programs/coe/indicator_cha.asp

4   Is Higher Education Disruptable?

The idea of disruptive change (Christensen, 1997) has become so embedded in everyday discourse about technology and industry that it is easy to lose sight of the radical nature of its central thesis. Disruption occurs when innovators in an industry offer a new product or service that is initially inferior to that of market leaders, but which gains acceptance by virtue of greater convenience, lower cost, or other features. Over time, the new product or service improves to the point that it fully displaces older versions, and incumbent market leaders are toppled. Disruption in industry is the equivalent of revolutionary regime change in the political arena. It is signaled by the rise of insurgent competitors who eventually overtake and dethrone traditional leaders, like a game of king of the hill. Those traditional leaders are made vulnerable by institutional inertia; they are unwilling or unable to change completely enough or fast enough to avoid being overtaken. Many observers of higher education (Selingo, 2014; Carey, 2016; Craig, 2015), including (Christensen & Eyring, 2011; Christensen et. al., 2015), have argued that American higher education is a prime candidate for disruption. The emergence of online learning and the unbundling of educational services, in particular, have been regarded as innovations that number the days for traditional colleges and universities. The theory of disruption implies that, in the field of higher education, those traditionally sitting on the top of the hill—in this case, flagship public and elite private institutions—are vulnerable to being displaced by newer institutions that represent very different approaches to education.

As we have already seen, there is a good deal of *prima facie* evidence to suggest that disruption theory, at least in its fullest sense, does not apply to higher education. Consider that U.S. News and World Report's first ranking of universities in 1983 incudes mostly the same top institutions as in more recent years—and no disruptive newcomers (Boyington, 2014). Beyond that, history shows that traditional institutions of higher education, and especially those at the top of the reputational hierarchy, have demonstrated remarkable staying power, not just for decades but, in some cases, for centuries. Such resilience is a sign of adaptability to social and economic change, not rigidity. Although there is a great deal of recognizable continuity across the higher education system over time, there have also been profound changes in the missions and structures of institutions. These are not signs of an industry vulnerable to disruption, at least if the past is any guide. However, we are often told that we live in times of unprecedented change. The question to which we now must turn is whether the resilience of higher education will continue in the face of the new demands of today.

In this chapter, I argue that patterns of disruption do not apply to higher education, for several reasons. The first reason is simply because industry leaders do not seek market dominance or exercise market power in ways that disruption theory requires. Therefore, the playbook for would-be disrupters is not likely to work. There are, however, additional reasons to expect that higher education will avoid disruption. These include the tendency to accommodate organizational innovation rather than to isolate and reject it, as well as the ability to incorporate innovations in both educational missions and service models. These traits of academia, which have supported its resiliency in the past, are likely to continue despite the increasing intensity and velocity of change in today's world.

Market Dominance and Market Power

Disruption theory is inextricably linked to the concepts of market dominance and market power. A dominant firm is one that controls the major share of a market. Such dominance reduces competitive pressures, which in turn gives a dominant firm unusual market power, especially to control pricing. If a firm has few major competitors, it can set prices that yield greater profits than would be the case in a more competitive environment. The extreme version of market power appears in monopolies, in which all competition is eliminated and there are no restraints on prices. The assumption is that all firms aspire to as much market power as they can accrue. Incumbent leaders want to retain and control market power, while disrupters want to take it away from them.

Competition in the higher education jungle, it may be easily observed, operates under very different assumptions. To begin with, there are no dominant institutions if that term refers exclusively to market share. American higher education serves roughly twenty million students each year, but no single institution enrolls more than a small fraction of this number. At their height, a few of the new generation of online institutions grew to several hundred thousand students, but most have since retreated to enrollments in the one hundred thousand range (McKenzie, 2018). Meanwhile, a large public university like Ohio State may enroll sixty thousand or so students, and an elite private research institution will likely have one-third to one-half that number. Holding a commanding market share, meaning enrolling a double-digit percentage of total enrollments, seems beyond the scope of any current institution, and it is not even a strategic goal of any elite university.

Indeed, the most prominent and successful institutions use their standing in the market to limit or reduce enrollments, even as the number of applicants rises. The most telling expression of dominance in higher education is the percentage of an institution's applicants who are *denied* admission. Among the most elite institutions, the admit rate is well below ten percent. Thus, the institutions that are most able to attract "customers" decline to serve more than ninety percent of them. This behavior is unimaginable in commercial enterprises.

If the most important privilege that comes with market dominance is the power to control pricing, here again, the most prestigious universities defy expectations. While the rise of tuition rates is a complicated and contentious issue, top-tier universities almost all calibrate the actual price paid by students based on their individual ability to pay. As a result, there is virtually no such thing as "the" price of attending a college. Wealthy universities devote a large percentage of their resources to offsetting the so-called "sticker price" through a variety of discounting methods. The net price actually paid by a student is a function of family income and savings. For example, a student from a family of four with one child in college, with an income of $100,000, can expect to pay about $11,000 for a year at Harvard, where the nominal cost of attendance (tuition, fees, room, and board) is more than $72,000 per year in 2018. At Williams College, where the total cost of attendance is nearly $74,000 per year, a similarly situated student might expect to pay $10,000 in net out-of-pocket costs.[1]

Not all institutions can afford to offset as much of the sticker price for students from modest means, but most provide at least some financial aid to all but the wealthiest students. According to the College Board, the average published cost of attendance among all four-year private colleges was $46,950 in 2017–18, while the average net cost (after scholarships and tax benefits) was $14,530 (College Board, 2019). Among public four-year institutions, the average total cost of attendance is $20,770, while the average net cost is $14,940. One might argue that these costs are still too high for many families, and they result in graduates who are overburdened with debt. This is a critical issue that must not be overlooked. For present purposes, however, the point to be made is a different one. Traditional colleges and universities do not seek to maximize their pricing power. To the contrary, the more elite the institution, the more likely it is to deeply discount its prices— all the way to zero—for admitted students with limited ability to pay. It does not have to be this way: If an elite institution chose to do so, it could almost certainly fill its annual classes with "full pay" students; it could even auction spaces and award them to the highest bidders if its goal were to maximize tuition income. The fact that all of the top institutions eschew such practices may well be the result of pragmatic calculations of self-interest as much as the result of academic convictions or altruism. Regardless of their reasons, the willingness to leave revenue on the table undercuts many would-be disruptors' abilities to compete aggressively on price. In point of fact, net costs at an insurgent online, for-profit institution are frequently higher than for a comparable degree program at a traditional institution.

Exclusivity is a critical factor in the business model of elite universities and colleges. The fewer applicants the institution accepts, the greater the value of admission becomes as the result of basic laws of economic scarcity. While this could translate directly into higher tuition prices, elite schools essentially forego immediate transactional income to increase future donations. Alumni are motivated to donate, even though they have no obligation to do so, in the interest of preserving the exclusivity and brand value of the membership they acquired as students. This virtuous cycle (from a business standpoint) grows stronger with each annual repetition. For new competitors seeking to draw away market share, it is nearly impossible to find a chink in the armor of dominant institutions. Furthermore, as we have seen from the Sweet Briar case, the basic mechanisms of this brand allegiance persist well down the reputational pecking order. Brand identity—or "academic reputation" in the preferred language of universities—is a strong force in the economics of institutions, and something that is difficult for insurgent institutions to create *de novo*.

To summarize, if disruption is meant literally as the displacement of market leaders by insurgents, it is nearly impossible to occur in higher education for the two reasons given above. First, there are no dominant leaders who control a disproportionate share of the market. Second, the most prestigious institutions decline to use their position to exercise market power, especially with regard to pricing. It is difficult to imagine the alternative value proposition that a would-be disrupter could offer in order to directly challenge the preeminence of elite colleges and universities.

Adopting Innovations

One might argue that the theory of disruption as applied to higher education does not so much target any single market leader, but instead threatens a broad range of practices that are associated with traditional colleges and universities, particularly among those most commonly regarded as industry leaders. In this modified view of disruption, what is at risk is an entire class of institutions that find it difficult to change their practices and business models in order to meet the needs of today's students. There are several characteristics of such putatively hidebound institutions that are often thought to leave them vulnerable. These include a failure to adopt new technologies to make teaching more scalable and efficient, unaccountable faculty members, and lack of innovation in the curriculum. The assumption is that these are deadweights from which traditional colleges and universities are unable or unwilling to escape. Here again, however, higher education tends to defy the expectations of disruption theory.

We have already seen that one way in which higher education adapts to changing environmental conditions is by spawning new organizational types. This allows academia at large to accommodate an increasingly varied set of missions and methods—but this is just part of the story of adaptation. It is also true that as new approaches arise in new institutions, they often spread across the entire academic enterprise. Let us consider some examples.

Online Learning

The first and most visible example of adaptation is online education. The late 1990s and early 2000s were extraordinary times for any activity touched by—or potentially touched by—the internet. It was during this period that many of us first began to use online services and could perhaps begin to glimpse of their power to alter or replace longstanding business models. Google, Amazon, and Facebook became household names, and the services they offered occupied increasing amounts of our attention, while traditional industries from publishing to retail sales were suddenly at risk of collapse. Trend spotters could begin to see what most of us barely understood: that whole ways of life would soon be transformed by online activity.

This frenzy was certainly felt in educational circles. While every new innovation in telecommunications—from motion pictures to television—has spawned predictions about transformations in the delivery of education to the masses, the internet has certain features that make it especially relevant for teaching and learning. Unlike broadcast technologies, the internet enables genuine interaction among groups of people. It also allows for relatively low-cost ways to reach enormous numbers of students, while giving them greater control over the time and pace of their experience. Among educational early adopters, these features were seen as important pedagogical advantages, even over conventional "face to face" classes. For investors, education looked like the next "killer app." One Silicon Valley CEO was quoted as saying that online education would someday reduce email to a rounding error in internet use statistics (Farrelly, 2014).

Such enthusiasm was not universal on college and university campuses, to be sure. Many professors viewed online teaching with suspicion, if not open hostility. It was seen variously as an assault on academic standards and a threat to the entire teaching profession. Surveys showed a consistent gap in acceptance between faculty members and university leaders, the latter being more likely to see institutional benefits and new sources of revenue (Parker, Lenhart, & Moore, 2011). Nevertheless, building an online presence was an expensive proposition, and few traditional college presidents had either the resources or the political capital within their institutions to pursue online education aggressively.

This was not a constraint on the burgeoning for-profit higher education industry. The most visible for-profit institution was the University of Phoenix, (UoP) established by John Sperling in 1976. Sperling was a faculty member at San Jose State University, and his initial idea was to create a company to invest in and manage adult-oriented extension programs on behalf of traditional institutions. This was proposed as a way both to expand educational opportunities for working adults and to create auxiliary revenue streams for colleges and universities. When Sperling sought accreditation for his programs, he was rebuffed by the accrediting commission with jurisdiction over California, and so he relocated to Phoenix in order to come under the purview of an alternative accrediting agency. With the move came a more ambitious and independent vision: Sperling would no longer focus on providing services on behalf of traditional institutions, but would instead concentrate on building a fully independent institution bearing the name of its new hometown (Sperling, 2000).

UoP grew rapidly by focusing on a student market that was neither well served nor well understood by most colleges and universities. By the late 1970s, the number of well-paying jobs that did not require a college education was already beginning to decline, and many working adults began to realize that they needed further education to stay competitive. These students, however, were not like the 18 to 22 year-olds who populated most college campuses. They often could not attend classes during the day and had no patience for the slow-moving pace of the traditional academic calendar. Furthermore, they were interested in obtaining skills and knowledge with immediate application to work. The dreamy life of the mind encouraged by most colleges was neither attractive nor possible for many adult students. Sperling realized that catering to this population required a complete transformation of the traditional service model of higher education. He offered classes in the evening, with frequent starts during the year. He offered the classes near clusters of employers, usually in office parks located near major freeways. Soon, University of Phoenix signs were visible on

office buildings in most major cities—a brash affront to traditional academia, with which Sperling was now in open competition.

UoP was not the first institution to explore online technology, but by
the mid-1990s it had fully embraced the idea. Online education enhanced
UoP's major value propositions: convenience and ease of access. Enrollments grew beyond the conception of any traditional institution, reaching a
peak of 470,000 students in 2008 (McKenzie, 2018). At the same time, new
online institutions began springing up, fueled by investors who were eager
to imitate UOP's success. By 2010, more than 12 percent of American college students were enrolled in a for-profit institution (Center for Analysis of
Postsecondary Education and Employment, 2019), and the majority of them
were studying primarily online.

While many faculty members on traditional campuses regarded the rise of
".com" universities the same way they would regard weeds in a garden, online
learning nevertheless also began to take root alongside the ivy. Experiments
with online courses sometimes began in extension and continuing education
departments in traditional institutions. Gradually, departments nearer to the
core began experimenting with new technologies. Many universities established offices of learning technology to help support early adopters among
the faculty, and hired new staff members with skills in online course design
and development. The enrollment tide began to shift. While the number of
students taking at least one course online has increased each year overall, the
number of online students enrolled at for-profit institutions has declined each
year from 2012 to 2016, while online enrollments grew fastest each year at
traditional public institutions, and to a lesser extent at private nonprofits (Seaman, Allen, and Seaman, 2018). In 2018, the fastest growing online institutions in the country were two private not-for-profit (albeit unconventional)
institutions: Western Governors University and Southern New Hampshire
University; and Arizona State University (McKenzie, 2018). Perhaps the most
visible signal that traditional universities successfully defended themselves
against the barbarians at their gates was the 2017 acquisition of for-profit
and online Kaplan University by Purdue University, a land-grant institution
founded in 1869 (Fain & Seltzer, 2017). Although the acquisition was controversial among Purdue's faculty, it nevertheless represented a kind of capitula-
tion of the insurgents, and the symbolic end of any serious threat that online
"big box" institutions would dominate the higher education landscape.

In retrospect, the online revolution in higher education represents just the
kind of novel response to new environmental conditions that organizational
ecology predicts of successful industries. Institutional diversity allowed for
experimentation, which in turn led to a level of acceptance across much of
the academic landscape. Although there was no strategic mastermind who
can claim credit for it, traditional higher education effectively got private

investors to finance much of the early experimentation with online learning, and then took over the innovation when it was cheaper and easier to do so. Even if higher education was more formally organized and coordinated, it is difficult to imagine how a more successful defense against the threat of the for-profit, online industry could have been mounted.

Reductions in Faculty Power

When critics list the ills of higher education, they often cite problems with motivating faculty members to be more efficient, accountable, and responsive to the need for change. Tenured faculty members live a rarified existence: They are among the very few workers with guaranteed lifetime employment, and there are few limitations on what they can say or do, even in contradiction to their employers. Their formal duties seem, on the surface, to occupy only a small fraction of a normal work week; they are well paid, often well-traveled, and afforded honors and respect. When Socrates was convicted of the "crime" of living a life of the mind, he facetiously proposed as his punishment that he be housed and fed at the public's expense for the rest of his life. Faculty members at today's elite universities and colleges can seem to many outside academia to have achieved what Socrates was unable to convince the Athenian Senate to do back in 399 B.C.

We have already seen that faculty power became institutionalized in American higher education in the early twentieth century, in tandem with the rise of the new PhD-granting institutions. This was partly due to basic laws of supply and demand. The establishment of so many new institutions created a seller's market for highly qualified faculty, and they began to be courted as individual stars rather than as replaceable cogs in the academic machinery. Faculty prestige also rose in parallel with that of other professions, including medicine and law. New professional societies helped define and solidify the hold of these professions over certain domains of practice, often reinforced by state licensing laws. Professionals became "sovereign" within these domains—they could not be second-guessed or overruled by lay people—and their professional organizations became self-regulating. Professionals became a kind of learned aristocracy in an otherwise democratic society. University professors came to enjoy much of this same status, in part because they were responsible for training those entering the learned elite (Friedson, 1986). Unlike other professionals who are often self-employed, however, university faculty depended on their institutions for compensation. Nevertheless, they succeeded in carving out broad areas of autonomy—similar to professionals in private practice—within their organizations. In academic circles, this political power is known as "shared governance," meaning that faculty stand alongside the president and board of trustees in overseeing the affairs of the institution. Contrary to widespread belief among many faculty members, shared governance does not mean that faculty have a voice in all decisions of the institution; instead, it means that faculty have nearly abso- lute authority over the academic domain (curricula, academic policies, the appointment of faculty colleagues, etc.), while the university's board and administration have authority over other areas, such as financial manage- ment (Association of Governing Boards, 2017).

For would-be innovators in higher education, faculty autonomy is a prob- lem to be solved, for two reasons: First, it is taken as a given that no orga- nization can function at maximum efficiency when a group within it has the power to resist or block management directives. The idea that a chief execu- tive should have to negotiate corporate strategy, or share control over the organization's major products (in this case, academic programs) is anathema, especially to investors who demand decisive leadership. There is little room in modern management theory for the notion that collaboration and delibera- tion lead to better outcomes if they come at the expense of clarity and speed.

The second reason many innovators seek to break the power of the faculty is cost. In most traditional colleges and universities, instruction is the most expensive line item in the budget. Most nonprofit and public institutions devote 40 percent or more of their annual budgets to teaching according to data sup- plied to the federal government. Furthermore, if faculty members are tenured or on long-term contracts, they represent a fixed cost, not subject to short-term fluctuation with enrollments. When combined with non-academic staff, com- pensation and benefits often equal up to eighty per cent of a traditional institu- tion's budget. Few businesses operate with such a high level of fixed personnel costs built into their operations. Not surprisingly, perhaps, investors do not tend to view the faculty's role as sacrosanct. To the contrary, the idea that each faculty member should devise his or her own courses is seen as inherently inef- ficient, the academic equivalent of craft work. As in the manufacture of goods, reformers have sought to move teaching to a mass production model. This has resulted in the reorganization of academic work in large-scale, big box institu- tions. In most new, for-profit institutions, a small group of academic leaders devise the curriculum, which is then "taught" by course leaders (who may or may not have traditional academic training), all reading from a common script.

This new model has greatly reduced both the role and number of aca- demic professionals in some innovative institutions. Whereas elite colleges or universities maintain student to faculty ratios of about 1:10 (plus or minus a bit), only about 1,000 faculty members had "any real say over what was taught" (Blumenstyk, 2015, p. 105) at the University of Phoenix when its enrollments totaled 250,000—a faculty to student ratio of 1:250. The Uni- versity of Ashford, another large online institution built on the Phoenix model, reported to the Securities and Exchange Commission in 2016 that it employed just 140 full-time faculty members to serve 45,000 students (Bridgepoint 10-K, 2016), a ratio of 1:321. These ratios mean that the cost of instruction at some large-scale institutions both plummeted as a percentage of total operating costs—to 10 percent or less—and became variable costs that could rise and fall quickly in response to enrollment changes.

Finding lower-cost means of production is a classic move in the disruptor's playbook because older, established institutions are frequently unable to change their practices quickly or radically enough to keep pace. In the case of higher education, the traditional faculty model remains well entrenched in elite institutions, but the costs of faculty are often borne to a considerable extent by restricted endowments or research grants. In other words, much of the faculty expense budget is covered by revenues that are earmarked for that purpose and that cannot be used for anything else. They are therefore not seen as a burden on general revenues. Across the academic industry as a whole, however, the role and cost of the faculty *has* been greatly diminished. According to the American Association of University Professors, fewer than one-third of instructors are tenured or in a tenure-track position, and more than 40 percent are in part-time, non-tenure-track positions (Curtis, 2014). College and university teaching for many new PhDs has become part of the gig economy, with instructors cobbling together careers made up of multiple temporary and part-time jobs. The surplus of underemployed academics has led to a complete transformation of the academic job market, with power now firmly on the side of the employers. While tenured positions at elite institutions continue to be highly paid, average earnings among all people with qualifications for the professoriate have plummeted.

The rapid erosion of both political power and earning power of the faculty amounts to an assault on a core belief among many academics, best captured in a classic economics paper by William Baumol and William Bowen (1966). The premise of the theory—sometimes called the cost disease—is that certain kinds of labor-intensive activities are resistant to efficiency gains if quality is to be maintained. A metaphor for this concept, which appears in the Baumol and Bowen paper—is a string quartet. One cannot reduce the workforce of a string quartet and expect to play four-part music with the same fidelity. Nor can one perform the music twice as fast in order to get two bookings per night instead of one, or play everything twice as loud to reach larger audiences. Any of the standard ways to increase productivity leads to degradations in the quality of the performance. Furthermore, if the musicians want to maintain their standards of living over time, they need steady pay increases each year. Thus, the quartet seems locked into an inescapable dilemma: costs will rise, with no way to gain efficiency. This same dilemma has been seen by many as applying to education. One cannot teach faster, or louder, or to ever larger class sizes, without eroding quality, and yet costs must rise.

The trend toward part-time instructors in higher education represents a response to the cost problem. There are many who argue that it carries the risk of degradation exactly as predicted by Baumol's theory, but others contend that efficiencies in the traditional teaching model are possible without a collapse of quality. For one thing, technology has substantially changed both the delivery of information and the role of the teacher. One no longer needs to rely on a learned professor to deliver knowledge that only he or she possesses. Most likely, that knowledge is readily available from other sources. As a result, the instructor serves more as an advisor in the learning process than as the sole font of wisdom. A popular saying in academia is that we've gone from the "sage on the stage" to a "guide on the side." Furthermore, many institutions have found value in hiring "guides" who bring practical experience into the classroom, not just formal knowledge, creating still more downward pressure on the market value of instructors educated at the doctoral level.

As we saw in the case of online learning, one cannot identify a single point of origin for the strategy of reducing faculty numbers and power across all of higher education. Indeed, it is a strategy only in hindsight; one can detect in national trends certain common—and perhaps inevitable—responses to changes in the academic job market, in the economics of institutions, and in the rise of new opportunities created by technology. The response to these environmental factors shows, once again, that higher education as a collective is adaptive—if not always intentional—in navigating change.

New Student Demographics

A third area of adaptation to explore is in the demographics of the students served by colleges and universities. This is another area in which many common assumptions about higher education are out of date with current realities.

The word "college" conjures up idyllic images for many of us: four years of intense and (ideally) mostly pleasant experiences, from late night bull sessions in the dorm to leisurely afternoons sunning on manicured campus lawns. Colleges are utopian in design and, to a considerable extent, in practice. They are artificial communities that emphasize most of the highest aspirations of human existence: the nurturing of curiosity, pursuit of shared interests, mutual respect, comfort, safety, and broad expanses of unconstructed time. Perhaps the best advice a commencement speaker could give to graduating students is: "Don't do it!—stay here!" There may be no other better existence than life as a carefree, full-time undergraduate on an American college campus.

If this is one's mental image of academic life, it will come as a surprise to read the following passage:

> The "traditional" undergraduate—characterized here as one who earns a high school diploma, enrolls full time immediately after finishing high school, depends on parents for financial support, and either does not work during the school year or works part time—is the exception rather than the rule. In 1999–2000, just 27 percent of undergraduates met all of these criteria. Thus, 73 percent of all undergraduates were in some way "nontraditional." Comparable data for a generation ago are not available, but the fact that much of the change in demographic characteristics and enrollment patterns described above occurred in the 1970s suggests that this is not a recent phenomenon.
>
> (Choy, 2002, p. 1)

Almost imperceptibly, American colleges and universities have moved from catering primarily to full-time students in their late teens and early 20s, to a student body comprising mostly older students juggling careers and families along with their educations. Furthermore, these students tend to dip in and out of college, often taking courses from more than one institution as they work toward a degree. More than sixty percent of recipients of bachelor's degrees have academic credits from two or more institutions (Complete College America, 2014).

This shift has done much to transform college and university campuses across the country. Many institutions now offer the majority of their courses in the evening to accommodate students with jobs. Most students commute to and from classes, and thus have little time or interest in many of the trappings of college life. Dormitories, clubs, and social activities, and even athletic teams are of little use to older students; indeed, "non-traditional college-goers view the social aspects of college life as distracting" (Deil-Amen, 2015, p. 144). Together with the trend toward more part-time faculty, many campuses serve less as idyllic residential communities and more as meeting points for people on the move.

These changes in campus life have important implications for the substance of education. Much of the rhetoric of higher education—the story it likes to tell about itself—has to do with the unfettered exploration of great ideas and the pursuit of new discoveries. Almost any college brochure will extol the "life of the mind" and the opportunities provided for deep intellectual engagement. Students are almost always encouraged to follow their curiosities and sample broadly from the range of courses and disciplines offered by the institution. But the reality of higher education for the majority of students has become far more transactional and instrumental.

Busy, working adults do not have the luxury of aimless wandering in the groves of academe. They want to know what it takes to move through a degree program in the most efficient manner possible. They grudgingly endure so-called general education courses, which are required by virtually all accredited institutions, and as a result, these courses are often desultory experiences. Students are eager to get on with accumulating academic credit specifically relevant to job interests, and they are concerned about spending time and money on anything else.

The growing misalignment between student interests and academic ideals has led to a sort of crisis of confidence in some parts of the academy, most notably the humanities. Departments of Art, History, Philosophy, and Literature feel increasingly marginalized on many campuses, losing enrollments to more practical disciplines such as computer science and business. The basic premise of liberal education is undermined by an increasing emphasis on career preparation rather than on intellectual cultivation. While this may represent a false dichotomy, many colleges and universities have responded with ambivalence, still extolling the higher intellectual purposes of education while simultaneously trying to cater to ever-more practical minded students.

Underlying the tensions between aspirations and reality on many campuses is a more basic shift toward the consumer. Many academics steadfastly resist referring to students as "customers." They are loath to reduce the relationship between teachers and students to a mere commercial transaction. Furthermore, it is fundamental to the notion of education that the student—unlike the customer—is not always right. By definition, the student does not know what he or she needs to know—and so, comes to the institution to learn. It is contradictory to the aims of education, therefore, to think that one should always yield to customer preferences and demands. Yet, colleges and universities have had to yield in many ways, and they increasingly find themselves competing for students on consumerist grounds. All but the most elite institutions, which still attract far more applicants than they seek to enroll, must market themselves on terms that speak to the interests and needs of prospective students. This often means putting an emphasis on career preparation, the availability of courses on demand, convenience, and other "non-academic" values.

As we shall discuss in Part II, efforts to shift the purposes of higher education to more practical goals may be self-defeating in the long run. For now, however, it is enough to observe that the majority of colleges and universities have responded to external economic and political forces by transforming their programs and services, however incompletely, to serving a new clientele. This is an ongoing transition, but one that has already been transformative on many campuses.

Catering more explicitly to working and part-time students has also allowed may institutions to fend off threats from new competitors that specialize in the adult education market. As we have seen, this was the core focus of many large scale for-profit institutions, which saw opportunities in a market that was largely ignored by traditional providers. Classic disruption theory predicts that incumbent leaders ignore encroachments by new competitors at the edges of their markets; the leaders are willing to cede segments of the market that are less profitable or less central to their business models. Early forays by new competitors such as the University of Phoenix fit this pattern precisely. However, as an industry, higher education has not ignored nontraditional students. Once again, it has responded to a change in the environment not by some well-coordinated, industry-wide strategy, but rather through cumulative local decisions made on hundreds of individual campuses. As a result, the adult learner, who was once a fringe interest of higher education, has become increasingly central to its mission.

The Big Tent of Accreditation

The foregoing discussion of responses to various environmental challenges suggests a pattern of accidental (i.e., unintentional and unorganized) effectiveness within the higher education enterprise. While there is no organizing structure to the academy, and therefore no uniform strategy, there are nevertheless industry-wide responses at critical moments. Education historian David Labaree (2017) has called American higher education "a perfect mess"—a haphazard collection of institutions that are successful in spite of the lack of a coherent system. The responses to disruptive threats described above illustrate at least part of what he meant: it is an "unsystematic system" that produces and sustains a large number of excellent institutions.

As noted earlier, the United States is nearly unique among nations in not having a coherent higher education policy. There are no national standards for what universities must teach or how they must be organized and administered. In fact, the national government does not even define "university" or "college." Many states do have such definitions and standards, but not all do.[2] Thus, in some parts of the country, almost any organization can call itself a university. To the extent that there are any *de facto* prevailing standards for higher education, they are indirectly administered through a complex system of accreditation. This system, which is at best an "imperfect mess," plays a critical role in higher education's collective ability to absorb change and respond to new environmental challenges.

Accrediting societies first appeared in the United States as early as 1885 (Brittingham, 2009). These were voluntary associations intended to promote quality and define—by membership—legitimate educational institutions from fraudulent ones. This was made difficult in part because of the lack of standards, even in nomenclature. One of the first tasks of accrediting societies was to sort out the differences among "academies," "institutes," "seminaries," and assorted other institutional names. There was also interest in creating better coordination between high schools and colleges to assure that students were well prepared for the transition between them. These early educational associations had no formal status, either in setting legal policies or in enforcing standards, except through peer pressure. Furthermore, they were regional associations, so different geographic sections of the country developed different approaches to describing and monitoring educational standards.

The federal government had no particular reason to be interested in setting standards for higher education until it began pouring money into the system, first through post-World War II education programs for veterans (the GI Bill), and later with the establishment of federally backed student loan programs. Because these programs provided grants to individuals who could use them anywhere, for the first time it began to matter to the government whether a "university" was a legitimate education provider or merely a diploma mill. Rather than create a new bureaucracy to develop and enforce standards, the federal government turned to existing regional associations. It effectively deputized them as gatekeepers, giving them authority to determine which institutions could qualify for receiving federal student loans and grants.

There are hundreds of accreditors, many of which specialize in particular programs or types of institutions (e.g., the American Bar Association oversees law schools). For purposes of this discussion, however, so-called "regional" accreditors are the primary focus. There are six such regional associations, five of which have names that pretty well identify their area of coverage: New England, Middle States (the mid-Atlantic area), Southern, Northwest, and Western. The sixth regional accreditor, based in Chicago, covers a vast area that includes the upper Midwest, the plains states, and parts of the Southwest. It is large enough to defy any single geographic descriptor, so it adopted the Higher Learning Commission as its name.

Participation in the accrediting processes overseen by the commissions is, in theory, voluntary; although since they determine eligibility for participation in federal financial aid programs, virtually all institutions are compelled to join. Each commission is governed by a board, made up of faculty members, administrators, and trustees from member institutions. These boards create standards for evaluation and decide on the accreditation status of member institutions based on periodic reports from the institutions themselves, as well as occasional visits from teams that are also made up of faculty members and administrators from other institutions in the region.

Thus, the evaluation process is a peer-based, self-regulated system, in which member institutions review and approve each other's accreditation status. Critics of this system contend that this is all far too clannish, if not incestuous, and does not allow for sufficient transparency, independence, and public accountability. Defenders of the system argue that only academic professionals are qualified to judge the effectiveness of academic institutions, and that member institutions have strong incentives to take seriously their responsibility for policing their own ranks.

Although accrediting commissions have the power to remove accreditation from institutions, this happens relatively infrequently. The loss of accreditation—and resulting loss of eligibility for federal financial aid programs—would be tantamount to a death penalty for almost all institutions. Thus, even questionable institutions are often given plenty of time and latitude to correct deficiencies and come back into compliance, and when the removal of accreditation is threatened, political and legal battles ensue. The slow and sometimes forgiving process reflects one of several dilemmas inherent in the accreditation system, in this case the tension between the interests of students (for whom closing an institution would be costly and disruptive), or other stakeholders, and the need to uphold standards. In 2012 The City College of San Francisco was in danger of losing accreditation due to chronic financial and governance problems. The result was a power struggle between the accreditor—in theory a private, voluntary membership organization—and a taxpayer-supported institution operating under the aegis of state law (Fain, 2012). The standoff took several years to resolve, during which the College apparently took sufficient corrective steps to resolve its issues with the accreditor. It was an example, however, of the fragmented regulatory regime under which higher education operates, and the lack of clarity over where accountability lies, and to whom.

Arguably, accrediting commissions exercise their greatest power in determining which new institutions qualify for initial accreditation. This, too, is a lengthy process that requires new applicants to demonstrate compliance with accrediting standards over a period of years before becoming fully accredited. For entrepreneurs and visionaries seeking to start new educational institutions, accreditation is the single highest barrier to entry. For this reason, accreditors are often seen by critics as impediments to innovation (Horn & Dunagan, 2018). A more objective view is that this is another area of tension inherent in the accrediting system, between promoting creativity and new approaches, on the one hand, and upholding standards, on the other.

To illustrate this point more fully, I can draw on my experience as a commissioner of the Western Senior College and University Commission (WSCUC, but usually known as "WASC"), which oversees accreditation for California and Hawaii. One particular episode is especially relevant. In 1997, Governors Michael Levitt of Utah and Roy Romer of Colorado agreed to join forces in the creation of a new institution that came to be known as Western Governors University (WGU). The two governors were interested in finding new ways to develop the workforces in their states without substantially adding to the cost of existing public university systems. WGU was conceived of as a radical experiment in competency-based learning, where degrees would be awarded based on the demonstrated mastery of knowledge and skills rather than on the number of academic credits earned. In its original design, WGU would not offer courses itself. Instead, it would test and certify students' competencies by whatever means they were acquired. Students might have taken courses at one or more colleges or universities, or have acquired on-the-job training, or even been self-taught. WGU's sole function was to validate the mastery of various competencies.[3]

From an accreditation standpoint, WGU presented two kinds of challenges. The first was procedural. Because of the quirks of regional accrediting boundaries, Colorado and Utah are under different jurisdictions. Colorado is a part of the Higher Learning Commission's territory, and Utah is part of the Northwestern region. Furthermore, several other states expressed interest in joining the WGU consortium, which potentially drew other accrediting commissions into the picture. For the first time, therefore, an ad hoc interregional commission was created to receive and consider WGU's application. WASC was a part of this interregional commission, and I served as one of its representatives.

The second challenge presented by WGU was more substantive. In its early conception, WGU proposed offering no traditional classes in its own name, and therefore it would not employ faculty members in the traditional sense. WGU's primary responsibility was to develop instruments to evaluate competencies, not to teach courses. However, the standards of each of the accrediting commissions assumed that all legitimate institutions employed faculty instructors. Indeed, sufficiency of faculty—qualified faculty members in each discipline, and the appropriate number to accommodate the student body—was a bright line indicator of institutional quality and integrity. A university without faculty was, for most of us, unimaginable.

The ad hoc committee of accreditors that was assembled to consider the special case of WGU debated many issues, but the most vexing of these was the faculty question. The accrediting standards generally relied on evidence of resource sufficiency as the main criterion for quality. The bottom line question for accreditors was this: "Does the institution have enough faculty, staff, books, facilities, and money to deliver on its educational promises?" For example, in the days before online information resources, it seemed to most accreditors to be an absolute necessity that each institution have a library with enough breadth and depth in its collection to support student research. Accreditors also wanted assurances that institutions had enough financial resources to avoid sudden cash flow problems or worse, bankruptcy. However, at about the same time that WGU came along, many accreditors had begun exploring ways to shift the focus of accrediting standards from inputs (e.g., the resources available to use in providing education) to outputs: evidence that showed how well an institution was achieving its academic mission.

Within the arcane world of academic accreditation, the shift from inputs to outputs was a revolution of Copernican significance. It arose from good intentions: accreditors were, by my observation, genuinely interested in reforming the system and in looking for better indicators of quality than by simply counting faculty noses and library books. But it was also clear that institutions such as the University of Phoenix and WGU were testing the limits of the old accrediting model. Although the full impact of the internet was still some years away, the idea of dismantling traditional institutional forms was certainly in the air. Accreditors, to their credit, began to recognize the pressures on their systems that were likely to arise, and to anticipate responses to those pressures. At the same time, their hands were being forced by political forces that had grown impatient with the pace of change in higher education and its apparent lack of accountability. WGU's political power was overt; members of the interregional committee all understood that if they failed to craft a solution for the new institution, its founding governors, who had powerful allies in the federal government, would bypass the accreditors altogether and obtain special dispensation from the Department of Education in Washington. This was seen as a grave threat to the entire system of accreditation. Suddenly, the idea of a faculty-less institution began to seem plausible. The participating accrediting commissions ultimately crafted language that allowed for academic supervision of WGU's competency-based system without the standard reference to faculty that existed in each of their separate standards. Similar language was soon thereafter incorporated into WASC's own accrediting rules, as well as in those of other regional accreditors. The current WASC standard includes a "criterion for review," rather than a firm regulation, which suggests that institutions should be "staffed by sufficient numbers of faculty qualified for the type and level of curriculum offered" (WASC, 2013). Thus, the faculty requirement is relative rather than absolute, and it can be tailored to the institution's educational profile. This change in fundamental accreditation standards has undoubtedly contributed to the decline in full-time faculty numbers and faculty power discussed above.

Accrediting bodies are extensions of the collaborative and collegial culture that exists in much of higher education. This is a product of both their history as voluntary associations and their structure of peer-based overseers. It is a quite different approach from that of, say, financial auditors, who are trained to evaluate business practices against a set of independent standards created by the auditing profession, not by those under scrutiny. To their critics, accrediting bodies often fail to act with sufficient independence and firmness. Peer review, to many of these critics, is just so much mutual back scratching—not a serious effort to police and penalize institutions for quality failures.

On the other hand, the structure of the accrediting process does allow for professional discretion that is not common in more rule-bound regulatory regimes. Financial auditors are seldom in a position to entertain innovations in accounting practices as "interesting experiments." To the contrary, unconventional accounting practices are often met with severe punishment: consider the infamous case of Enron and its auditor, Arthur Andersen, neither of which survived their experiments with creative accounting. Accreditors have greater ability to grant institutions a measure of latitude around the standards if they—as peer educators—are persuaded that the intentions behind the innovation have academic integrity. This flexibility helps to create conditions for experimentation and innovation within the borders of higher education and, therefore, allows for the diversity of institutional types that we have seen as critical to the adaptability of the overall system. It is difficult to imagine the variety of educational missions and methods that characterize American higher education existing under a stronger external authority.

Note that this argument does not suggest that all experiments and innovations are positive for the academy or its students. One might argue that allowing WGU to weaken faculty oversight was an abrogation of the responsibility to uphold standards and, by normalizing a bad idea, a disservice to the entire academic community. However, competency-based education is a well-established pedagogical approach that many educators see as fully legitimate. To the extent that WGU was a radical experiment, it was in the attempt to structure an entire institution around this one central idea. It seems contrary to the aims of education to deny that new approaches and methods deserve to be explored and tested. From the perspective of institutions interested in preserving their role as arbiters of quality and integrity, it is better to conduct these explorations within the academic community than to invite competing systems to pitch their tents outside the walls.

A criticism one sometimes hears of colleges and universities is that they all suffer from "Harvard envy" (Christensen & Eyring, 2011). That is, every institution aspires to be like the richest and most prominent university in the land by emulating its range of programs, supporting research as well as teaching, producing PhD students, and attracting superstar faculty. Of course, very few universities have the resources necessary to succeed in this imitation, so the attempt nearly always falls well short of its intended goal. What is less often observed is that institutions look both up and down the academic hierarchy for ideas. Harvard has committed substantial resources to developing online programs—something it learned to do in part by observing fully online institutions at the opposite end of the academic hierarchy. Big universities learn about building student communities from small colleges, for which the richness of student life is essential to success. Public universities have increasingly learned from private ones about how to cultivate and develop donors in order to replace declining state subsidies. Almost every institution that must compete for students has been forced to learn about telemarketing, online marketing, social media, and other tools of the recruitment trade that were developed most energetically by for-profit institutions. In higher education, very few strategic advantages last for long; they are too easily replicated by other institutions. Good ideas—or necessary adaptations—tend to be shared broadly and quickly, in every direction. Accreditation helps to legitimize many of these experiments within the academic community, and thus becomes a way of propagating innovation.

The academic community is as prone to fads and fashion as any other social organization, and undoubtedly it is vulnerable to false prophets. At the same time, colleges and universities operate with a great amount of inertia. They change course reluctantly and with difficulty, and this has been to their benefit. The accrediting regime that has arisen almost by accident serves to maintain a kind of porous border between legitimate experimentation and educational hucksterism. It does so imperfectly, but the benefits of this imperfect system almost certainly outweigh its risks.

The Potential for Regulatory Disruption

The theory of disruption is usually understood as referring to competition among firms. In higher education, for reasons discussed above, it is difficult to imagine a new entrant in the market succeeding at overturning the hierarchy of institutions that has been firmly established for more than a century. However, there are risks to elite institutions that come not from competition with newcomers, but rather from reliance on a regulatory regime that sustains their business models. The federal government could cause dramatic changes to the established order—intended or otherwise—by making relatively modest changes in policy, specifically in three areas: taxation of endowments, indirect costs on research, and support for student loans.

Taxation

The most distinctive common feature of elite colleges is the size of their endowments relative to their financial operations. Among the eight Ivy League universities, for example, investment returns average 43 percent of total annual revenues per institution (calculated from institutional data available from U.S. Department of Education IPEDS data base). Endowment management involves the art of balancing short-term demands to support current expenses against the goal of maintaining or growing the fund in perpetuity. Returns on most investments are not subject to tax, which helps provide a margin between income and outflow that allows for reinvestment and growth in real terms (i.e., growth beyond inflation.)

The major tax bill passed by Congress in 2017 imposed a small tax on investment returns at institutions with at least $500,000 of endowment capital per student. While the impact of this new law is limited to only about thirty-five institutions, it breached a long-honored separation between the nonprofit world and other parts of the economy. Historically, lawmakers have steered clear of encroaching on the wealth of charitable institutions, including private colleges and universities, in recognition of the public benefits they provide. The 2017 tax was seen by many university administrators as shot across the bow—a warning that the deference traditionally afforded to charities may no longer be granted to institutions that have accumulated enormous wealth. If this is but a first shot, and if Congress comes to regard endowment returns in general as a new source of tax revenue, the impact on institutions could be profound.

Tax expenditures (i.e., foregone taxes) are by far the largest form of public subsidy to higher education, and they go disproportionately to highly endowed, elite institutions. According to a 2015 study by the Nexus Research and Policy Center, the indirect support afforded through tax exemptions greatly exceeds even the amount of direct subsidy given to public institutions (Klor de Alva & Schneider, 2015). The authors of the Nexus study calculate that tax exemptions per student for the ten most highly endowed private institutions were worth nearly three times the average direct allocation per student at public institutions in the same states.

The Nexus report argues for the creation of an excise tax on large endowments and a transfer of the proceeds of that tax to subsidize students at public institutions. This is a radical proposition in itself, in that it amounts to commandeering funds given in trust to one institution and distributing them to another, but at least one might argue that it would be done in the broader service of education. In point of fact, Congress adopted only half of the Nexus proposal, implementing the tax without the recommended transfer to other students. If this practice were to be expanded, it would erode an important line between for-profit and nonprofit entities. There are numerous potential consequences, including disincentives for donors to give new funds. The accumulation of wealth by elite colleges and universities has been made possible by a regime of trust upon which donors have relied, and which has in turn produced a collection of extraordinarily strong institutions. The risk of undermining this system is high, and the consequences are potentially severe.

Indirect Costs for Research

A second policy shift that would disproportionately affect elite institutions could arise in the area of government funded research. As noted earlier, after World War II the federal government chose to continue investing in university research as a strategy for building a national research and development capacity that has proven unmatched anywhere in the world. Universities have strong incentives to seek research funding, not only because it brings the prestige of discovery to faculty members, but also because the funding helps defray substantial overhead costs. A sharp reduction in so-called indirect cost recoveries (i.e., allowances for administrative and capital expenses) would handicap universities with large research infrastructures, especially in the medical and physical sciences.

University scientists obtain research funding through competitive, peer-reviewed processes managed by federal agencies such as the National Science Foundation and the National Institutes of Health. Research proposals contain detailed budgets for salaries, equipment, and other costs necessary to conduct the project. In addition, each proposal contains an indirect cost rate, which functions as a surcharge on direct expenses. Large institutions negotiate specific indirect cost rates that can be 50 or 60 percent of the direct cost budget. Smaller institutions may accept a generic rate. On average, for every dollar of research funding awarded by the federal government, about thirty cents goes for indirect costs. These funds help to build and sustain the infrastructure required to support research, including a share of the institution's general costs for administration, computing, libraries, facilities, and so forth.

Other kinds of entities, such as private foundations, also provide funds for university research, many of which pay little or nothing toward indirect costs, and this has caught the attention of federal policy makers. For example, the 2018 budget proposal from the Department of Health and Human Services includes a proposal for standardized rates that would effectively reduce indirect cost payments and enable the government to spend more on direct research. While this is proposed as a way of freeing institutions from the burden of documenting and defending specialized rates, it is another implicit threat to an established paradigm that has guided research funding for decades. Shifting more indirect costs onto university base budgets would have a particularly large effect on institutions with medical centers, where some of the most expensive research takes place (U.S. Department of Health and Human Services, 2018). As with the change in tax law above, there are substantial risks in changing a system that has been so demonstrably successful for many decades.

Student Loans

A third area of exposure to regulatory disruption is in the area of federal student loan funding. Student loan programs have taken on a highly charged political valence as the federal loan portfolio has grown to $1.5 trillion and has become the bedrock of many institutions' financial structure. Very few colleges and universities could sustain their current budgets without relying on tuition income financed through federal loans to students. Critics of these loan programs claim that they both provide unintended price support for colleges and universities, and encourage unreasonably high debt levels for students. Some warn of a massive debt bubble bursting, much like the mortgage crisis in the early 2000s (Kaletovic, 2018). The student loan regime is often characterized as an unwarranted subsidy to elite and inefficient institutions, creating unsustainable debt levels for borrowers and a huge exposure for taxpayers.

Proposals for reform through several presidential administrations have focused mostly on subsidy levels and repayment options for borrowers, including income-based payment plans and loan forgiveness after a certain number of years. There have been few serious proposals to eliminate the government's role as the primary lender entirely, although there have been calls for changes that would force colleges and universities to share risk. One such proposal (Chou, Looney, & Watson, 2017) would track repayment and default rates by institution. If repayment rates fell below a specified threshold, the institution would reimburse the government for a portion of the unpaid loans. The purpose of such a reform would be to give institutions a greater stake in the employment and economic outcomes of their students.

As a matter of public policy, institutional risk sharing will strike many as a reasonable way to hold institutions accountable for the benefits they receive from taxpayer-supported investments in higher education. As a matter of educational policy, it would force many institutions to strengthen career-oriented programs and respond rapidly to shifts in employment markets. As we shall discuss in Part II of this book, this may be a self-defeating strategy. Most colleges and universities are not well designed to follow rapid changes in the economy, nor should they be. Attempts to become more responsive may, ironically, weaken institutions and reduce their resilience.

Unintended Consequences

The greatest disruptive threats from policy changes are those that are both counterintuitive and unintended. Federal higher education policy in the U.S. has evolved as a patchwork of programs that lack strategic coherence. The only policy goals we have are *de facto* ones: to encourage private support for institutions through tax policy, to support high quality research, and to support student access and mobility through loan programs. Few discussions of programmatic reform address these derived policy goals explicitly, and thus there is danger that they can be unintentionally undermined. Colleges and universities have evolved for more than seven decades under a relatively stable policy regime. Sudden changes to this regime would undoubtedly put stress on the system overall, with differential effects on specific institutional types. As in any industry, weak, and marginal institutions are the most vulnerable. It remains likely that flagship institutions (those with the most resources and strongest reputations) would be best positioned to survive sudden policy changes, although they could also be severely stressed. It is not clear that any reasonably foreseeable set of policy changes would substantially overturn the present hierarchy of institutions in ways that the theory of disruption predicts. Nor, however, is it clear that the kinds of "reforms" often discussed among critics of higher education would do anything positive for the best institutions, nor produce any greater benefits to the public.

Conclusion to Part 1

The burden of the first part of this book has been to show that the diversity of organizational forms and academic missions that exist within American higher education is a source of great strength. This diversity has arisen in response to environmental challenges and opportunities, and has resulted in the unusual co-existence of institutional types. The academic industry is loosely organized and regulated, which allows for continuous experimentation and evolution. Some innovations tend to spread broadly among institutions, while others remain as specialty niches or die away altogether. In sum, the flexibility of the overall system has enabled it to respond to new social and economic demands as they arise. None of this has been particularly intentional, if by that term one means having been guided by a central strategic authority. If there is genius in the system, it is as much the product of accident as design.

I have tried to avoid making normative judgements in the forgoing discussion. My purpose has been to show that change happens, and explore how it happens. The direction of change maybe positive or negative, but that is another discussion altogether. To return to the language of organizational ecology, the standard of evaluation is "fitness" for the environment, and by this standard we can say that American higher education has been remarkably successful. The question we shall turn to in Part II is whether there is reason to believe that this success will continue; whether the kinds of environmental change we can foresee in the near future will overwhelm the adaptive capacity of colleges and universities. These questions also avoid normative issues, except in one important respect. I take it as a given that formal higher education is both a public and private good of the highest order. The survival of institutions dedicated to providing higher education is therefore something to be highly valued. I hope in the following pages to show how colleges and universities can continue to play a vital role in a rapidly changing society and economy.

Notes

1. These figures are from "net price calculators" available on each institution's website.
2. New York is one such state that regulates the use of the term "university." Hence the state's response to Trump University in 2016, which the state said was not entitled to call itself a university.
3. Since its early days, WGU has changed its educational model. Although it still places heavy emphasis on competency-based learning models, students must earn credits by taking online courses offered by WGU in order to earn credentials and degrees.

Bibliography

American Association of University Professors. (2015). *Trends in the academic labor force, 1975–2015*. Washington, DC: American Association of University Professors. Retrieved from www.aaup.org/sites/default/files/Academic%20Labor%20Force%20Trends%201975-2015.pdf

Association of Governing Boards. (2017). *AGB board of directors' statement on shared governance*. Retrieved from www.agb.org/statements/2017-1010/agb-board-of-directors-statement-on-shared-governance

Baumol, W. J., & Bowen, W. G. (1966). *Performing arts, the economic dilemma: A study of problems common to theater, opera, music, and dance*. Cambridge: MIT Press.

Blumenstyk, G. (2015). *American higher education in crisis? What everyone needs to know*. Oxford: Oxford University Press.

Boyington, B. (2014, September 9). Infographic: 30 editions of the U.S. News best colleges rankings. *U.S. News and World Report*. Retrieved from www.usnews.

com/education/best-colleges/articles/2014/09/09/infographic-30-editions-of-the-us-news-best-colleges-rankings

Bridgepoint Education, Inc. (2016). *Annual report pursuant to Section13 or 15(d) of the securities exchange act of 1934 for the fiscal year ended December 31, 2015*. Retrieved from http://d1lge852tjjqow.cloudfront.net/CIK-0001305323/93de762b-6fb0-43e3-ad36-6067cb9b2ee1.pdf

Brittingham, B. (2009). Accreditation in the United States: How did we get to where we are? *New Directions for Higher Education*, (143), 7–27.

Carey, K. (2016). *The end of college: Creating the future of learning and the university everywhere*. New York: Riverhead Books.

Center for Analysis of Postsecondary Education and Employment. (2019). *For-profit colleges by the numbers*. Retrieved from https://capseecenter.org/research/by-the-numbers/for-profit-college-infographic/

Chou, T., Looney, A., & Watson, T. (2017). *A risk sharing proposal for student loans*. Washington, DC: The Brookings Institution, The Hamilton Project. Retrieved from www.hamiltonproject.org/assets/files/risk_sharing_proposal_student_loans_pp.pdf

Choy, S. (2002). *Nontraditional undergraduates: Findings from the condition on education, 2002*. Washington, DC: U.S. Department of Education and Institute of Education Sciences, National Center for Education Statistics. Retrieved from https://nces.ed.gov/pubs2002/2002012.pdf

Cole, J. R. (2009). *The great American university: Its rise to preeminence, its indispensable national role, why it must be protected*. New York: Public Affairs, a Member of the Perseus Group.

College Board. (2019). Average published undergraduate charges by sector and by Carnegie Classification, 2018–19. *The College Board*. Retrieved from https://trends.collegeboard.org/college-pricing/figures-tables/average-published-undergraduate-charges-sector-2018-19

Complete College America. (2014). *Four-year myth make college more affordable: Restore the promise of graduating on time*. Indianapolis: Author. Retrieved from https://completecollege.org/wp-content/uploads/2017/05/4-Year-Myth.pdf

Christensen, C. M. (1997). *The innovator's dilemma: When new technologies cause great firms to fail*. Boston: Harvard Business School Press.

Christensen, C. M., & Eyring, H. J. (2011). *The innovative university: Changing the DNA of higher education*. New York: John Wiley & Sons.

Christensen, C. M., Raynor, M. E., & McDonald, R. (2015, December). What is disruptive innovation? *Harvard Business Review*. Retrieved from https://hbr.org/2015/12/what-is-disruptive-innovation

Craig, R. (2015). *College disrupted: The great unbundling of higher education*. New York: St. Martin's Press.

Curtis, J. (2014). *The employment status of instructional staff members in higher education, fall 2011*. The American Association of University Professors. Retrieved from www.aaup.org/sites/default/files/files/AAUP-InstrStaff2011-April2014.pdf

Deil-Amen, R. (2015). The "Traditional" college student: A smaller and smaller minority and its implications for diversity and access institutions. In M. Kirst &

M. Stevens (Eds.), *Remaking college: The changing ecology of US higher education*. Stanford: Stanford University Press.

Fain, P. (2012, July 6). Something has to give. *Inside Higher Education*. Retrieved from www.insidehighered.com/news/2012/07/06/accreditation-crisis-hits-city-college-san-francisco

Fain, P., & Seltzer, R. (2017, April 28). Purdue's bold move. *Inside Higher Education*. Retrieved from www.insidehighered.com/news/2017/04/28/purdue-acquires-kaplan-university-create-new-public-online-university-under-purdue

Farrelly, T. (2014). E-learning and higher education: Hyperbole and reality. In A. Loxley, A. Seery, & J. Walsh (Eds.), *Higher education in Ireland*. London: Palgrave Macmillan.

Friedson, E. (1986). *Professional powers: A study of the institutionalization of formal knowledge*. Chicago: University of Chicago Press.

Higher Learning Commission. (2019). *About the higher learning commission*. Retrieved from www.hlcommission.org/About-HLC/about-hlc.html

Horn, M., & Dunagan, A. (2018). Innovation and quality assurance in higher education. *Christensen Institute*. Retrieved from www.christenseninstitute.org/wp-content/uploads/2018/06/accreditation_alana_final_final.pdf

Kaletovic, D. (2018). *The $1.5 trillion student debt bubble is about to pop*. Retrieved from www.nasdaq.com/article/the-15-trillion-student-debt-bubble-is-about-to-pop-cm976619

Klor de Alva, J., & Schneider, M. (2015). *Rich schools, poor students: Tapping large university endowments to improve student outcomes*. San Francisco: Nexus Research and Policy Center. Retrieved from http://nexusresearch.org/wp-content/uploads/2015/06/Rich_Schools_Poor_Students.pdf

Labaree, D. (2017). *A perfect mess: The unlikely ascendency of American higher education*. Chicago: University of Chicago Press.

McKenzie, L. (2018, April 23). The 100K club. *Inside Higher Ed*. Retrieved from www.insidehighered.com/news/2018/04/23/nonprofits-poised-unseat-u-phoenix-largest-online-university

Parker, K., Lenhart, A., & Moore, K. (2011). The digital revolution and higher education: College presidents, public differ on value of online learning. *Pew Research Center*. Retrieved from https://files.eric.ed.gov/fulltext/ED524306.pdf

Seaman, J., Allen, I., & Seaman, J. (2018). *Grade increase: Tracking distance education in the United States*. Babson Research Group. Retrieved from http://onlinelearningsurvey.com/reports/gradeincrease.pdf

Selingo, J. (2014). Innovation in 2014: Welcome to the evolution. *The Chronicle of Higher Education*. Retrieved from www.chronicle.com/article/Innovation-in-2014-Welcome-to/143971

Sperling, J. (2000). *Rebel with a cause: The entrepreneur who created the University of Phoenix and the for-profit revolution in higher education*. New York: Wiley.

U.S. Department of Education, Institute of Education Sciences, National Center for Education Statistics. (2017). *Institutional postsecondary education data*. Washington, DC: Author. Retrieved from https://nces.ed.gov/ipeds/use-the-data

U.S. Department of Health and Human Services. (2018). *HHS FY 2018 budget in brief*. Washington, DC: Author. Retrieved from www.hhs.gov/about/budget/fy2018/budget-in-brief/index.html

WASC Senior College and University Commission. (2013). *Standard 2: Achieving educational objectives through core functions: In the 2013 handbook of accreditation.* Alameda: Author. Retrieved from the WASC www.wscuc.org/resources/handbook-accreditation-2013/part-ii-core-commitments-and-standards-accreditation/wasc-standards-accreditation-2013/standard-2-achieving-educational-objectives-through-core-functions

Part II

5 Neither Pangloss Nor Quixote

We saw in Part 1 that higher education has responded repeatedly to three external stimuli to change: new social demands on colleges and universities, the availability of capital from new sources to finance innovation, and the emergence of new organizational models that can be adapted to academic goals. When these three forces align, the past tells us that new kinds of institutions will emerge—and that they will join their predecessors in altering the higher education landscape. The question for Part 2 of this book, therefore, is how these patterns of past innovation will shape the future of colleges and universities. I will argue that we can already see the outlines of the next wave of innovation.

Before taking up this next part of the discussion, I want to forestall at least one possible misunderstanding of my thesis up to this point. By asserting that higher education has successfully navigated a range of external environmental changes, I do not mean to suggest that colleges and universities are therefore without weakness or fault. Nor do I want to echo Voltaire's (1759/1975) Dr. Pangloss, who said, "There is a concatenation of events in this best of all possible worlds." There are indeed concatenations of events and social forces at work that shape academia as we know it today, but this is not to say that we have the best of all possible higher education systems. Many areas call out for improvement: Tuition prices are too high for most students, and as we have seen, the federal loan program creates perverse incentives for both borrowers and institutions. Elite institutions could do more to identify and support talented, underrepresented students striving to move up the socioeconomic ladder (Chetty, Friedman, Saez, Turner, & Yagan, 2017). College athletic programs distort the values of too many institutions and, in some cases, exploit student-athletes. Faculty members are often too resistant to changes that would be in the best interests of their institutions, their students, and the communities they serve. And, despite the oft-heard refrain that American universities are the best in the world, a more accurate assessment is probably that the United States has far too broad a range of academic quality, and tolerates too many weak and inadequate institutions that do not serve their students well, and that tend to exacerbate inequality rather than help ameliorate it. (Clotfelter, 2017; Mettler, 2014). These are serious indictments of the existing system of higher education that, if left unaddressed, will further erode confidence in even the strongest institutions. Panglossian complacency is among the greatest risks of the existing higher education regime.

Where there are reforms to be made, reformers will surely appear—and higher education attracts many, each of whom who is "spurred on by the conviction that the world needs his immediate presence," as Cervantes (1616/1986) says of his hero, Don Quixote. Many of those most energetic in the effort to bring about change—the reformers, the disrupters, the entrepreneurs, and the visionaries—are often poorly informed about the institutions they seek to upend. As a result, they are easily dismissed by the traditional academy as being unrealistic and insufficiently appreciative of the core strengths of the institutions they want to replace. They may be effective provocateurs, but seldom are they able to build institutions with staying power. A corollary of my thesis of adaptive change is that environmental forces play a larger role in shaping higher education than do the visions of academic crusaders. Moving an institution, and *a fortiori* an industry, requires the collaboration and cooperation of many participants, both inside and outside of its walls. It also requires a deep understanding of the multiple forces, challenges, and purposes of education. Leadership is seldom singular and heroic, and lasting change is seldom sudden. Charging off to battle against imaginary demons is of no more lasting value to the goals of academic excellence and institutional effectiveness than is resting on the laurels of past achievements.

Impatience with higher education often stems from a sense that it refuses to fully embrace the present moment. Universities are seen as havens both for those who want to dwell in the past, and for those who dream of idealistic and unrealistic futures. These are seen by many as indulgences that are no longer worth their cost, if they ever were. Academia is being challenged to demonstrate its intrinsic value to an increasingly skeptical public. This challenge constitutes one of the most important environmental forces that will give rise to a new wave of change.

Higher education enjoys what Louis Menand calls a "delicate and somewhat paradoxical relation" (2010, p. 158) to the broader culture. This relation is one in which academia flexes and responds to society, but does not merely reflect its passing trends and fashions. Higher education does a disservice to society if it only seeks to satisfy customers and affirm conventional wisdom. We rely on colleges and universities to be institutional gadflies at the same time we expect them to be relevant and engaged with issues of the day. Neither Pangloss nor Quixote are well suited to the subtleties of this relationship. Anachronistic irrelevance on the one hand and excessive zeal for currency on the other are opposite but equal threats to the ability of higher education to remain at the vital center of social and economic change.

Higher education's future challenges will be like the ones of its past. Institutions will need to determine how best to serve an ever-changing set of social and economic needs without falling into the ephemera of the moment. As new educational missions and structures emerge, they will, as they have in the past, challenge orthodoxy within the academic enterprise, but they will also retain proven customs and traditions that provide an overlay of continuity to underlying change. To quote Menand again, "Academics need to look to the world to see what kind of teaching and research needs to be done, and how to better organize themselves to do it. But they need to ignore the world's demand to reproduce its self-image" (2010, 158). We should neither expect nor desire that higher education fully embrace whatever fashions overtake other kinds of organizations and industries. The changes that we should hope to see emerge in higher education are those that arise in equal parts from self-criticism, careful deliberation, and experimentation. Few other institutions in society have the ability to manage change in quite this way.

Bibliography

Cervantes Saavedra, M. de (1547–1616/1986). *The adventures of Don Quixote de la Mancha*. New York: Farrar, Straus, Giroux.

Chetty, R., Friedman, J., Saez, E., Turner, N., & Yagan, D. (2017). *Mobility report cards: The role of colleges in intergenerational mobility*. National Bureau of Economic Research. NBER working paper number 23618. Retrieved from www.nber.org/papers/w23618

Clotfelter, C. (2017). *Unequal colleges in the age of disparity*. Cambridge, MA: Harvard University Press.

Menand, L. (2010). *The marketplace of ideas: Reform and resistance in the American university*. New York: W. W. Norton & Company.

Mettler, S. (2014). *Degrees of inequality: How the politics of higher education sabotaged the American dream*. New York: Basic Books.

Voltaire. (1759/1975). *Candide*. New York: Random House.

6 Education in the Age of Information

We have seen that new demands on higher education arise from time to time, resulting in new formulations of the mission of colleges and universities. For example, land-grant universities arose in part to respond to the need for practical arts education in fields such as agriculture and engineering. These subjects had not been considered "proper" for university study previously, but the rapidly expanding nation sensed that it needed builders, not (just) poets—and so these practical disciplines took their place alongside the traditional liberal arts, eventually appearing in the curricula of institutions even beyond those created by the Morrill Act. Higher education's scope has grown to accommodate the expansion of knowledge and the need for more specialized skills in the economy. It is reasonable to think that this expansion of the academic mission will continue as social and economic needs evolve. However, it is also clear that we are entering into a time of unprecedented change that will bring qualitatively different challenges for colleges and universities than they have faced in the past. The growth of information technology, particularly the growing impact of artificial intelligence in our lives, signals a profound change in our concept of knowledge and learning— and, therefore, in what it means to be educated.

The admittedly speculative task of this chapter is to explore how higher education may respond to an information-saturated, artificially intelligent future. Contrary to many of the reforms now emerging on college and university campuses, I will suggest that the most meaningful and lasting changes will not involve more focused preparation on careers. Instead, I submit that the future of higher education will depend on a renewed focus on higher intellectual capacities that are not as likely to be replicated or imitated by an "infosphere," made up of ubiquitous information and increasingly intelligent devices. The information age will put increasing pressure on a traditional fault line in higher education between vocational preparation, on the one hand, and intellectual pursuits, including basic research, on the other. Efforts to accommodate these two, often divergent purposes of education have always been awkward, and they are likely to become untenable. Higher education will face increasing pressures to plant itself firmly along one side of the widening fault or the other; straddling it may no longer be a successful strategy.

Ironies of the Information Age

The phrase "Information Age" first appeared in print in 1960 and is attributed to Richard Leghorn, a pioneer in aerospace spy cameras. I believe the previous sentence to be true because I entered the query, "who coined 'information age'?" in an internet search engine and this answer popped up within milliseconds. This is how the information age provides recursive proof of its own existence: It is Googled, therefore it is. The Internet's source for this tidbit of knowledge, however, is a much older technology: The Oxford English Dictionary (OED), which has been the authority on word origins since 1884. And if we were to trace the source of OED's entry for this phrase back even further, we would find that some now-anonymous researcher had to track down the first printed appearance of "information age," verify it, define it, and document it according to OED standards. The creation of knowledge does not come spontaneously or without effort, even if it soon becomes available to almost everyone with a few strokes of computer keys.

The information age does not so much herald the invention of something new—we have always had information—but rather the ease and speed of disseminating it. Had I wanted to know the origins of a word in earlier times, I would have had to know about the existence of the OED, and would most likely have had to go to a library to use it. That, in turn, would have required skills such as knowing where to find the correct volume on the shelf, or knowing how to ask a reference librarian for assistance, or even perhaps knowing some obscure term like "etymology." These skills and knowledge would have marked me as an educated person, for they are the kinds of personal capital—knowledge of the social conventions of libraries, vocabulary, and other literary and research skills—I would have picked up in school. A central purpose of education has been to cultivate in students a set of capabilities and habits focused on the acquisition of information. Before the internet, information was an expensive commodity because it was costly to obtain and difficult to manage and store. As a result, expertise—the mastery of knowledge about certain domains of information—has been the goal of much of formal schooling.

Information technology has reduced the cost of obtaining and storing knowledge to nearly zero. Now, it takes no more skill than the average grade schooler possesses to search for a fact online. Ironically, the information age designates a time when data—the raw material of knowledge—has become been virtually costless. At the same time, information has become increasingly valuable as a tool for other purposes, from basic research to marketing. This central paradox of the value of information in our time was captured presciently in a famous exchange in 1984 between computing pioneers Stewart Brand and Steve Wozniak that became a mantra of the technology age:

> On the one hand information wants to be expensive, because it's so valuable. The right information in the right place just changes your life. On the other hand, information wants to be free, because the cost of getting it out is getting lower and lower all the time. So you have these two fighting against each other.
>
> (Levy, 2014)

Information technology has also dramatically changed our personal and institutional relationships to knowledge, which has potentially profound implications for every level of education, from the elementary grades through graduate and professional training. In earlier times, an educated person might be said to have "owned" certain bodies of knowledge—if not exclusively, then at least on a highly privileged basis, and a university degree was a kind of deed of proof. The physician or lawyer or scholar knew things that others in the community did not, and therefore had a form of proprietorship over knowledge, just as the farmer or manufacturer owned capital assets. Today, almost all information is available to anyone with an internet connection, up to and including the most advanced subjects such as science and medicine, and so the idea of privileged access is fast disappearing. While few of us would dare to perform important medical procedures based on online information, many people now refer to medical websites to perform self-diagnoses and to research potential treatments. We no longer rely exclusively on a single authority for even highly technical knowledge. Information has been transformed from the personal asset of the expert to a nearly ubiquitous utility.

Higher education may also be losing its special institutional relationship to information. Just as the town doctor could be said to have owned knowledge in previous times, colleges and universities had a near monopoly on the production, collection, and dissemination of certain kinds of information, represented both by the books in the library and the knowledge "in the heads" of its faculty. Until recently, if you wanted to access to the world's most advanced and valuable knowledge, your only real option was to enroll at a university and to acquire it at the time and in the manner prescribed by it. A second irony of the information age, therefore, is that the one institution in society most clearly charged with producing and disseminating knowledge is at risk of losing its monopoly. This was evident, for example, in the short-lived frenzy over Massively Open Online Courses, or MOOCS (Daniel, 2012). For a few years in the early 2000s, it seemed to many observers that a handful of MOOCs could serve the world's hunger for knowledge with little or no human, much less institutional, intervention. These online courses were designed to serve millions of simultaneous learners, and they were offered almost entirely automatically; even the grading was done by machine. They took the concept of scale in education to an entirely new level, not only in terms of numbers of students but also in terms of its geographic reach and ease of access. Suddenly, new possibilities were within reach: an aspiring prodigy in rural India or Africa could learn from the leading scientists of the world, without going to the nearly insurmountable trouble and expense of traveling to and matriculating at a distant university. The institution was essentially cut out of the picture—a fact driven home when some faculty members began to leave prestigious university posts to establish startup companies devoted to producing and disseminating MOOCs. It seemed for a time that MOOCs might be that much-anticipated disruptive force in the knowledge business that would challenge the dominance of traditional universities.

Enthusiasm over MOOCs began to fade when it became apparent that very few people who signed up for them managed to complete them. It seemed that many people enrolled on an impulse—why not, if it was easy and free?—but found it too difficult or insufficiently interesting to stick with it. (Ubell, 2017). Completion rates as a percentage of initial enrollments fell to single digits. For those who did finish, they lacked the validation of an educational institution to certify their achievement. They may have gained knowledge, but they did not end up with a marketable credential.

The MOOC experiment has faded from view, but some companies that were founded to develop them continue to grow and evolve, in part by creating partnerships with traditional institutions that lead to various levels of certification (Young, 2017). While they are unlikely to become full alternatives to traditional colleges and universities, MOOC providers are pioneering new approaches to accessible, low-cost training, especially related to job skills. As such, they provoke new discussions about the relationship between education and work, and more importantly about the cost/benefit ratio of traditional education. Colleges and universities, then, cannot take their hegemony for granted when information can be easily packaged and distributed by other kinds of organizations. The idea that "information wants to be free" is a challenge not only to the business model of higher education, but also to the organizing principle that knowledge transfer must be carefully managed by academic experts. Indeed, in some forecasts of the future, (Schrager & Wang, 2017) professors themselves are on the endangered species list of occupations because it is imagined that teaching will be done by machines.

The Coming Infosphere

The most fundamental challenge to higher education that arises from the information age has to do with the core meaning and purposes of learning. No educator would contend that the simple intake of information constitutes learning. Rather, the purpose of education is to give students the ability to pursue and accomplish complex goals, and to use knowledge to inform their beliefs and actions. Until recently, these were thought to be exclusively human capacities that could be cultivated and improved through education. Today, even these higher intellectual ambitions seem open to challenge from increasingly sophisticated information technologies. Two innovations in particular—artificial intelligence and "neuromedia"—appear to signal important changes in the way we think about acquiring and using information.

Philosophers have been intrigued by the idea of thinking machines at least since the time of Descartes, but until recently their debates more mostly, well, academic. While it has long been possible to imagine machines that could function autonomously and at high levels of cognitive achievement, it has also been possible to postulate limits to their capabilities. Forty years ago, debates raged over whether computers would ever be able to play chess at the level of a grand master. That line was crossed in 1997 when IBM's Big Blue computer defeated world champion Garry Kasparov (Teicher, 2018). More recently, it was asserted that machines could never succeed at game such as Jeopardy, which requires much more open-ended knowledge and sophisticated semantic processing. That challenge was met in 2011 by another IBM computer called Watson (Markoff, 2011). And still more recently, a computer programed by Google defeated human masters of the Chinese game Go, which is said to be far more complex than chess (Mozur, 2017). While debates continue about the true meaning and significance of AI, it has becoming increasingly clear that there are no bright lines to distinguish between human and machine capabilities. To the contrary, it seems apparent that for any complex task, from driving an automobile to performing heart surgery, it is likely that a machine can be built to do it as well or better than a human can, given enough dedicated time and engineering resources. This is true up to and including the famous Turing Test, which was first proposed by computer science pioneer Alan Turing (1950). Turing proposed that if an evaluator cannot tell the difference between a human respondent and a machine respondent in a blind test, we must conclude that the machine is exhibiting the same intelligence as the human. Consider any test that can be devised, from language translation to running a psychotherapy session, and there are programs capable of meeting human standards, or there soon will be. We may still reasonably debate whether machines can have *true* intelligence or merely a facsimile of it, but for many purposes this ceases to matter. As Daniel Dennett (2007) has written, if you want to compete against a chess playing computer, you had better treat it as if it is an intelligent opponent that has the same goal-directed motivations as you. Underestimating either its "knowledge" of the game or its "desire" to win is a sure way to lose.

A second important development in information technology is the advent of what has been called "neuromedia," by some observers. Pritchard (2018) describes this near-future technology as "information-processing technology that is so seamlessly integrated with our on-board cognitive process that the subject is often unable to distinguish between her use of those on-board processes and the technology itself" (p. 328–329). In other words, instead of going to an external device such as a computer or cell phone to type in a query, neuromedia would consist of an embedded search-engine device of some kind that one could call upon in the same way as one's memory. Wearable computing devices with limited functionality are already available; fully developed neuromedia would extend the power of such devices and make them ever more intimately connected to our bodies. The true breakthrough will come from full integration with our natural mental processes. For those of us who wear eyeglasses (or better yet, contact lenses), it is easy to imagine a piece of equipment that improves and augments a natural capacity without our noticing it most of the time. A cognitive extension device would similarly provide fully transparent enhancements to our natural information-processing abilities.

Let us grant that artificial intelligence and neuromedia are both realistic technologies that will broadly and increasingly affect our lives in the near future. Extrapolating from current trends, we can easily imagine an environment in which a great many tasks in our households and workplaces are performed by smart machines rather than by humans. We can also imagine that most of the world's information is easily available virtually "at will." Such a world will of course dramatically affect social and economic ways of life, and there will inevitably be both positive and negative consequences. We can imagine a more egalitarian and leisurely utopia in which the technological environment will cater to our every need and desire. We can also imagine a dystopian world in which we become subservient to the machines we have imbued with intelligence. The chances are good that we will find ourselves in some middle position between these two extremes, and the next few generations of the human experiment will be greatly preoccupied with working out the challenge of harnessing and coping with new knowledge-enabled technologies. Among the issues that will be forced upon us will be the recalibration of the meaning and value of education.

Ever since the Industrial Revolution we have become accustomed to the idea that machines can replace human *labor*, and thus many low-skilled occupations such as assembly line work have already disappeared. Now we face the prospect that machines can also substitute for human *intelligence*, and so whole new categories of professions are potentially threatened, including so-called "knowledge workers," such as accountants, lawyers, and, as mentioned above, even college professors. The first line of concern for colleges must be related to their role in career preparation. Shrinking demand for humans in many knowledge-based occupations may erode the claim that higher education is a necessary step toward better jobs and higher earnings.

A second line of concern stems from the vision of neuromedia portrayed above. If anyone can access information by simply conjuring it up from a wearable or embedded device, there would seem to be no advantage to learning facts the old fashioned way. Nor would any privileged status be afforded to those who had "natural" command of a body of knowledge instead of "artificial" command. This would seem to obviate the need for spending considerable time and money attending school beyond the basic level required to comprehend the information available through neuromedia.

These are twin anxieties, therefore, that threaten to undermine much of the rationale for higher education. On the one hand, artificially intelligent devices will take over many of the positions that educated humans once occupied. On the other hand, spending time and resources on acquiring specific knowledge will be increasingly pointless because it will be widely accessible to nearly everyone. Thus, institutions in the "knowledge business" may find both their purpose and their customer base disappearing.

Turing 2.0

The Turing test was first proposed as a thought experiment to test our intuitions about what it means to be intelligent, albeit indirectly. Instead of trying to carefully define the similarities and differences between human cognitive capabilities and those of machines, Turing proposed what he called an "imitation game." The rules of the game are simple: If a machine can imitate a human well enough to avoid detection under blind testing conditions, it must have the same claim to intelligence as the human. The Turing test is not about intelligence per se, but about the functions (like responding to queries) that intelligence supports. If such functions can be performed by different kinds of systems (e.g., "natural" ones and "artificial" ones), we should regard them as equivalents. Just as important, however, the Turing test reveals the differences (if any) between artificial and human intelligence. That is, uncovering ways in which the machine fails to fully imitate human intelligence helps to define what it means to be humanly intelligent. In the early days of computing, it was fairly easy to expose machine intelligence by, say, asking semantically ambiguous questions. The significance of developments such as IBM's Watson computer lies in the fact that machines are becoming far more adept at dealing with such complexities, which apparently reduces the gap between humans and machines.

There is an equally interesting thought experiment to be conducted with respect to education in the information age: let's call it Turing 2.0. Imagine two humans, both of whom have access to all of the latest information technology available—high-powered computers with the most advanced algorithms, implanted neuromedia devices, powerful search engines, and so on. Imagine these devices not just as they are today, but as they may be in twenty or fifty years' time: an all-encompassing technological environment—an infosphere—that makes the world's information available with little or no effort, and that can not only retrieve information but use it in sophisticated ways.

Imagine further that one of the two humans in our thought experiment—Subject A—has no formal education beyond whatever is needed to use this new information technology. The other human—Subject B—has been to college—and perhaps even has advanced degrees in whatever discipline you may choose. With these conditions in mind, and to paraphrase the opening sentence of Turing's (1950) paper, I propose to consider the question, "Is there a difference between an educated person and a non-educated one in an artificially intelligent, information-rich environment?"

To start this discussion, consider another thought experiment in the literature on artificial intelligence that is nearly as much debated as the original Turing test: John Searle's Chinese Room (1999). Searle imagined a subject who knew nothing about the Chinese language, locked in a room with pages of Chinese text and a computer program for answering questions in Chinese. Note that this is not meant to be a *translation* program that renders Chinese into the subject's native language. Instead, it is a program that allows the subject to receive queries in Chinese, look up answers from the Chinese text, and send them back out as responses in Chinese. Let us further suppose that the "system," (i.e., the combination of the room, the texts, the computer program, and the human operator) functions well enough to answer questions that are indistinguishable from those given by a native Chinese speaker.

Searle argues that, although the person locked in the Chinese room might respond successfully to an unlimited number of questions (given enough reference materials), it would be wrong to say that he or she "understands"

Chinese. The element of understanding requires something other than symbolic processing capacity. Understanding requires cognitive capacities such as consciousness, awareness, and intentionality. The structure of the experiment deliberately mutes these capacities in the human subject. The person in the locked room functions as part of an algorithmic machine that processes inputs and outputs, but his or her "understanding" capacity has been essentially switched off. The lesson Searle draws from this thought experiment is that a computer processing system, no matter how sophisticated, lacks essential elements of mental experience that cannot be artificially created.

The poor person locked in Searle's Chinese Room is an extreme example of Subject A in my proposed Turing 2.0 test. It is someone who, we may presume, is adept at using information without comprehending it. This is merely an extrapolation of situations in which we all find ourselves, with increasing frequency. Educators used to worry about whether the introduction of electronic calculators would undermine their efforts to teach basic mathematical concepts because students would not need to have even basic understanding of computational functions to arrive at correct answers. Nevertheless, calculators are increasingly used even in elementary schools with the result that students are more adept at finding answers even as they (may) have less understanding of the operations they are performing. This trend toward ability without understanding is characteristic of increasing the amount of intelligence built into the infrastructures in which we work and live.

Let us return to the question posed by Turing 2.0: What difference, if any, would there be between the educated subject and the non-educated one in the infosphere of the future? In order to claim that there are differences, we need to be able to describe an "education premium" that would exceed the capacities of the non-educated user. Such capacities, however, are not likely to appear as differences in the ability to perform information-processing tasks, for the conditions of our thought experiment make it likely that both subjects will function equally well. However, just as we readily intuit the difference between an authentic Chinese speaker from the subject in Searle's Chinese Room, we also have intuitions about what it means to understand information—not merely use it. Let us call this domain of understanding the "intellectual virtues," a phrase that Pritchard also employs: "Intellectual virtues have a distinctive kind of value that contrasts them with mere cognitive abilities. They are to be prized regardless of their practical worth, for example, whereas mere cognitive abilities are usually only evaluated in terms of whether they serve our instrumental goals" (2018, p. 336). Thus, one promising area to look for differences between the two subjects in our Turing 2.0 universe will lie in intellectual capacities that are not delimited by the mere processing of information for specific tasks.

Intellectual Virtues

The phrase "intellectual virtues" is an implicit reference to Aristotle, who sought to categorize the various ways in which we acquire and use knowledge. He asked, how do humans come to know things? In response, he proposed five distinct ways:

> Let it be assumed that the states by virtue of which the soul possess truth by way of affirmation or denial are five in number, i.e., art, scientific knowledge, practical wisdom, philosophic wisdom, intuitive reason; we do not include judgement and opinion because in these we may be mistaken.
>
> (Aristotle, n.d.Nicomachean Ethics, 1139b, 15)

This passage is from one of the standard translations of Aristotle, although there has been much debate about the best way to capture his concepts in English. The first term in the list, art, is *techne* in Greek, and refers to a broad range of technical skills, craftsmanship, and artisanship. The unifying concept has to do with making and manipulating objects, materials, and tools to produce something. The artist or craftsman knows certain truths about the materials and tools he works with, as well as about techniques to reliably produce desired results. The carpenter knows that wood will split if it is nailed too close to the edge of the board; the violinist knows where to place her fingers and how to the draw the bow across her strings to sound a desired note on her instrument. Technical knowledge is the most common and widespread way of knowing about the world; it is the kind of knowledge that most people rely upon to make a living. While the Greeks regarded technical knowledge as both intellectually and socially inferior to more sophisticated pursuits, in modern terms, technical knowledge underlies many highly skilled and complex professions, from engineering to medicine. The common denominator that runs from carpentry to surgery is familiarity with certain materials, experience with how they respond to various treatments, and the kind of skills that are best honed by practice. Furthermore, this form of knowledge is often gained most effectively through apprenticeship and practice rather than through formal teaching.

Scientia, or scientific knowledge, is Aristotle's next category, and in this case the apparent similarity between the Greek and English words is slightly misleading. Modern science is defined primarily by a formal process for discovering and validating knowledge. The scientific method involves the formation of hypotheses, experimentation, and rigorous validation of results. Aristotle had no such well-defined process for scientific investigation, but he did practice systematic observation across a number of domains, from biology to politics. What he sought in these observations, and therefore what he means by "science," is the discovery systematic regularities in the world. It is, for example, one thing to observe that one heavy object falls to the ground when dropped. But if we notice that all heavy objects fall to the ground, we may have said to discover an abiding truth about heavy objects. This kind of fact-gathering and pattern detection is the first step in organizing useful knowledge about the world.

Aristotle's third way of knowing—"phronesis," in the Greek—is the most challenging to translate into a single English word or phrase (Noel, 2007). We are given "practical wisdom" in the translated passage above. It involves knowledge of how to get things done in the world, and more specifically, how to achieve desirable goals. There is a moral dimension to this concept, for "desirable" outcomes are those that are good in the full sense of that word. Thus, *phronesis* has also sometimes been translated as "moral insight," or "prudence." All of these translation options involve the capacity to discern right from wrong, as well as the ability to understand how one's actions help lead to either good or bad outcomes. This kind of knowledge is what allows us to plan our own lives and to be aware of the effects of our actions on others. For example, in the legal system we hold people most fully accountable for those things they intend to do purposefully, and for those outcomes that can be reasonably foreseen. Phronetic knowledge is what makes us fully responsible agents.

The fourth category of knowledge in Aristotle's taxonomy is *sophia*, or philosophical wisdom. This is the kind of knowledge that comes not from facts themselves, but from reflection about their significance. It is not only the province of philosophers, but of anyone who has ever wondered why things are as they seem, or whether there are deeper lessons to be learned from experience. Philosophic knowledge helps stitch together discrete experiences into a flowing narrative, and grants them meaning and significance. This is the kind of knowledge extolled by Socrates as the highest aspiration of the human mind. It transcends mere factual knowledge; indeed, as Socrates said with characteristic irony, his wisdom consisted in understanding that he knew nothing for certain. Thus, there is an enduring link between "sophistication" and skepticism.

The final way of knowing for Aristotle is by intuitive reasoning, or *nous*. This is intuitive, or immediate, knowledge that one simply "sees" with the mind's eye. We grasp logical truths in this way, for example, by understanding that if a=b and b=c, then a=c. There is very little one can do to explain this if one doesn't sense its necessary truth; it is a given, but it is not given to us by an external authority, but rather by the force of its self-evidence. Descartes would later call this kind of intuition "clear and distinct" knowledge that comes to us with such force that it cannot be questioned. However, the fact that knowledge of this sort is intuitive does not mean that it comes without discipline and training. Philosophers from Socrates to Dewey (1997/1910) argued that a primary function of education is to give students tools and discipline to discover self-evident truths—and to enable them to distinguish such truths from falsehoods posing as facts.

The final clause of Aristotle's passage is important because it provides two counterexamples to knowledge: judgement and opinion. Why do these not count as knowledge? Aristotle says it is because we may be mistaken in them; they are not reliable guides to truth. Indeed, neither of these are the product of intellectual discipline by themselves. We may hold opinions and make judgements based on no evidence, and indeed no thought process. We may also be easily swayed in our judgements and opinions by vagaries of the moment, which is a sign that they do no point us toward permanent truths.

Contemporary discussions about artificial intelligence often ignore the subtleties of Aristotle's categories. Intelligence is not just one thing; it is several. Some forms of intelligence, such as technical knowledge, are entirely instrumental; we acquire knowledge about how to manipulate materials and objects in order to accomplish tasks. As robots replace humans in manufacturing, they amply demonstrate their equivalence in the area of technical knowledge. Ever more powerful computers also now encroach on Aristotle's second category—scientific knowledge—by manipulating quantities of information that far exceed human abilities. From such massive data processing are revealed patterns and trends that could not otherwise be seen in domains such as climate change and epidemiology. While this use of information is not all there is to science, it does correspond closely to what Aristotle meant by that term. It is the knowledge that comes from empirical observation, with the goal of understanding the world by collecting and organizing data.

In these two areas, then, there is very clear potential for the two subjects in our Turing 2.0 test to perform equally well. Both of them could deploy mechanical and information tools to accomplish tasks, respond to inquiries, and perhaps even discover new truths about the world. To the extent that these are among the goals of education, it seems likely that new information-rich tools will eliminate the need for a great deal of formal training. We have, and will increasingly continue, to rely on the infosphere to perform tasks that require both technical knowledge and data manipulation because both of these forms of knowledge are oriented toward performance, even in highly complex situations.

It is not as clear that this may be said of the remaining intellectual virtues in Aristotle's taxonomy, none of which have the same kind of task-fulfillment orientation as the first two. As noted above, phronetic knowledge is difficult to translate, but it carries within it both managerial and moral aspects. A person with practical wisdom has the ability to deliberate about what goals are good for himself and others, and how to achieve them. Phronetic deliberations have a long arc to them; they have to do with how we choose to live our lives, how we choose to expend our energies and talents, and what goals we consider worthy. This requires both what psychologists refer to as "executive functions." (i.e., the ability to manage one's own cognitive abilities toward some goal) and also the social and cultural capital required to be effective in the world. This is not the sort of knowledge that aims toward the completion of a single task, but rather seeks to bring personal and social resources into alignment with a morally useful, often long-term goal.

Philosophical wisdom has a similar non-utilitarian character, except in the broadest sense of pursuing a worthwhile and fulfilling life. Aristotle's *sophia* refers to a range of intellectual habits that would include, among others, curiosity, reflectiveness, critical abilities, consistency, and diligence, among others. These virtues would not manifest themselves in straightforward computational processes, nor do they aim at a particular cognitive goal. Indeed, the value of this form of intellectual virtue is often thought to be in its pursuit, not in its outcomes. Philosophical knowledge, together with phronetic knowledge, lies at the core of what Socrates called "the examined life."

Finally, among Aristotle's intellectual virtues, there is intuitive knowledge. There are longstanding debates about whether such knowledge is truly possible, and if so, whether it derives from within ourselves (e.g., is a product of the way our brains are wired) or is a reflection of fundamental truths about the world. This is a debate we need not enter here, but we can observe that under either interpretation, intuitive knowledge is not the product of computation or algorithmic processing, but rather of some direct insight that seems to bypass more methodical processes of thought.

We therefore have at least three candidate intellectual virtues—phronetic, philosophical, and intuitive—that are neither narrowly instrumental nor narrowly computational in character. If Turing 2.0 successfully detected marks of education among subjects in information-rich environments, the evidence would consist of manifestations of these virtues. But this leads to the next question: How should education contribute to the development of these "organic" intellectual virtues?

The Liberal Arts and the Intellectual Arts

To the extent that there is an organizing principle of undergraduate education in American higher education, it is to be found in a common dedication to the liberal arts. The phrase "liberal arts" is itself an outmoded way to describe the curricula at most institutions, since it long ago ceased to designate any particular sequence of courses or disciplines, much less a coherent educational philosophy. However, virtually all institutions that award associate's and bachelor's degrees require students to sample courses in a range of disciplines from the humanities, social sciences, and natural sciences. Even if the faculty chafe at these requirements, as they often do, they are generally written into the standards for accreditation in the U.S. system. While these general education requirements are not identical to a full liberal arts curriculum, they stem from the same educational theory. Broad exposure to the disciplines, it has long been believed, enables students to appreciate diverse methods of inquiry and different fields of scholarship. Defenders of this approach will further argue that a broad exploration of the arts and sciences produces graduates who are flexible thinkers and creative problem solvers. The breadth of general education requirements, and the broader liberal arts curriculum of which they are a part, derive from an academic philosophy which holds that he value of education is not in the command of a body of knowledge or skills, but rather in the capacity to learn and adapt under a variety of circumstances.

For many critics of academia, the promised benefits of liberal education are insufficient (Deresiewicz, 2014). They argue that college curricula have become overburdened with trivia[1] and political correctness. Hence, the fundamental purpose of exploring broadly ("liberally") across the disciplines has lost both rigor and purpose, at best producing dilettantes instead of deep thinkers; at worst, forcing students through a bewildering array of choices for little discernible purpose (or perhaps worse yet, indoctrinating students into vaguely defined leftist political ideology that is often associated with humanistic disciplines). Other critics charge that the problem lies not with poor execution of the liberal arts approach, but with the very concept itself. According to this view, students need time to master subjects that interest them and that will repay their financial investment in education, not take a tour through the esoteric margins of academia. These critiques have led to substantial challenges for institutions devoted largely or exclusively to the liberal arts, but also at more comprehensive institutions that, as we have seen, must retain a semblance of general education for regulatory purposes. The prevailing disillusionment with the liberal arts has led to a siege mentality among departments in the humanities and social sciences whose lifeblood has been reduced to providing an unappreciated prelude to more technical and practical studies.

In spite of widespread impatience with the liberal arts curriculum, the conviction remains among many educators that it is the surest way to cultivate a broad set of intellectual virtues. A recent defense of the liberal arts, issued jointly by the American Association of University Professors and the

American Association of Colleges and Universities, makes essentially this point:

> The disciplines of the liberal arts—and the overall benefit of a liberal education . . . foster intellectual curiosity about questions that will never be definitively settled—questions about justice, about community, about politics and culture, about difference in every sense of the word.
>
> (2018)

In other words, the value of the liberal arts lies primarily in their lack of certainty, and in their willingness to engage in nuance and complexity. The nature of these questions requires Aristotle's higher intellectual virtues— moral wisdom and philosophical curiosity chief among them. And yet, in defenses of liberal education, these virtues are often seen as *byproducts* of the curriculum. They are desirable goals that, *it is hoped*, emerge from the various curricular foci available to students, but they are frequently portrayed as indirect goals.

The question begged by these sorts of apologies is, why not aim directly for these goals instead of treating them as byproducts? If the difference between being educated and being uneducated in the context of an intelligent infosphere is to be found in the higher intellectual virtues, how can colleges and universities prepare their students to fully distinguish themselves from their less-educated counterparts?

There are nascent efforts in higher education to move from the liberal arts to what I shall call the "Intellectual Arts," putting higher order intellectual virtues at the center of curricular goals. For example, Joseph Aoun (2017) argues that the implicit lessons of many traditional courses in the arts, humanities, and social sciences should be made more fully explicit:

> A traditional liberal arts program, for instance, might see professors leading students through rigorous consideration of gender in the Victorian novel while implicitly teaching strong writing and critical thinking skills. In our new model, teachers have to expose the underlying fabric of learning to their students, like turning a sweater inside out. They need to delineate clearly what is being studied, practiced, and acquired, explicitly identifying processes and goals in every component of a course.
>
> (p. 73–74)

Aoun proposes four cognitive capacities as forming the core components of an "inside out" curriculum. They are critical thinking, systems thinking, entrepreneurship, and cultural agility, all of which are (currently) beyond the capacity of even the most advanced artificially intelligent systems. Pritchard (op. cit.) offers an alternative, but similar, list of intellectual virtues that he argues should constitute the main goal of education, including epistemic autonomy, open-mindedness, and managerial control over one's cognitive skills. Both of these lists, as well as others (e.g. Baehr, 2011), point toward intellectual capacities that echo Aristotle's higher virtues. They have to do with the discernment and the evaluation of evidence, the direction of one's efforts toward useful goals, the curiosity and a willingness to engage with novel ideas, and the ability to bring about change by marshaling both social and physical resources in the environment.

Moving from the liberal arts to the intellectual arts offers an important avenue for colleges and universities in the age of technology. The value proposition for higher education must be in its ability to define and demonstrate an education premium of the sort that would emerge in Turing 2.0: a discernible difference between educated and non-educated denizens of the coming infosphere. The history of computing thus far suggests that there is no line in the sand that machines cannot—or will not—cross if the challenge is defined in terms of task-oriented capacities. To the extent that there remains a reserve of human talent that is unlikely to be replicated artificially, it is captured in a form of nuanced thought that motivates more questions than answers. In yet another irony of the information age, we continue to rediscover Socrates' ancient teaching that the essence of wisdom is not the *mastery* of information, but the recognition of its limits.

The increasing value of higher intellectual virtues offers a new niche for higher education, and an opportunity for experimentation with new missions. Specifically, institutions are likely to arise that emphasize "intellectual arts" rather than "liberal arts." This will involve a new definition of the essential goals of education; instead of an unstructured tour of various disciplines in the pursuit of a set of indirect benefits, curricula will be more carefully structured to lead to an education premium that holds its value in the new infosphere—those "inside out" results that Aoun argues will help make us "robot-proof." The new educated elite will be less likely to be associated with particular professions or bodies of knowledge, and instead will be those with capacities least likely to be replicated by artificial intelligence.

We have seen that new types of institutions arise when new social requirements emerge. At some moments of history in higher education, these new types of institutions have arisen *de novo*; such as the emergence of the land-grant institutions and the doctoral universities during the latter half of the nineteenth century. At other times, new institutional types have been built from existing ones, e.g., when doctoral universities became R&D contractors in the 1960s, and large public institutions transformed themselves to absorb new student demographics created by the GI Bill and federal loan programs. It seems likely that the coming changes in our conception of higher education will most profoundly affect existing liberal arts colleges, which have the opportunity to refashion themselves by leading the exploration of our new relationship to knowledge, information, and the moral issues arising from a world dominated by technology. In order to seize this opportunity, they will need to navigate strong headwinds that are pushing them toward more vocational missions. Contrary to current thinking on many campuses, it is a strategic mistake for traditional colleges to attempt to cater to the rapidly changing needs of employers. That work will be done by organizations that are purpose-built for the mission, and they will do it more efficiently than any traditional academic institution.

Higher education has long struggled to overcome the tension between two competing missions: intellectual growth and personal fulfillment, on the one hand, versus career preparation on the other. The most common response to this tension has been to settle for an unsatisfying compromise. The liberal arts and humanities are portrayed as having hidden, indirect utility in employment, while vocational programs are buried under layers of general education requirements and non-relevant electives. On both sides, the value proposition is obscured.

If the most radical forecasts about the future of work are to be believed, career preparation will be an increasingly difficult mission for traditional higher education institutions to fulfill. This is because the pace of change in the technical skills needed to serve employer's needs will be much faster than colleges and universities can cope with. It will make little sense to invest in the personnel, facilities, and curricula needed to train students in skills that will quickly become obsolete. The time scales for academic decision-making will be increasingly out of sync with employer demands. It will be much more efficient for employers to take over much of the responsibility for training their own workforces and create pathways for regular skill updates, as indeed some are now doing (Wang, 2018). To the extent that higher education attempts to continue to serve a career-preparation function, it will likely be in settings such as technical schools and highly specialized institutions, which, as we have seen, have long been part of the higher education landscape. These institutions have certain advantages over more traditional colleges and universities: they are amenable to having their training programs heavily influenced by employers; they tend to have fewer tenured faculty (whose own knowledge may become obsolete); and they have programs of shorter duration and faster throughput of students. For institutions unwilling or unable to adopt these practices, vocationally oriented programs will be increasingly uncompetitive.

The opportunity to refashion a nineteenth-century theory of liberal arts into a twenty-first century curriculum emphasizing the intellectual arts belongs not just to today's small colleges, but to the higher education enterprise as a whole. Those institutions that embrace this opportunity are the most likely to ride the next wave of innovation rather than be overtaken by it.

Notes

1. This is an intended pun. "Trivia" derives from the "trivium:" grammar, logic, and rhetoric, which were the first three subjects of the classical liberal arts curriculum.

Bibliography

Aoun, J. (2017). *Robot-proof: Higher education in the age of artificial intelligence.* Cambridge: MIT Press.

Aristotle. (n.d.). *Nichomachean ethics: Book VI* (W. D. Ross, Trans.). The Internet Classics Archive. Retrieved from http://classics.mit.edu (Original work published 1925).

Association of American Colleges & Universities, American Association of University Professors. (2018). *Joint statement on the value of liberal education by AAC&U and AAUP.* Washington, DC: Authors. Retrieved from www.aacu.org/about/statements/2018/joint-statement-value-liberal-education-aacu-and-aaup

Baehr, J. (2011). *The inquiring mind: On intellectual virtues and virtue epistemology.* New York: Oxford University Press.

Daniel, J. (2012). Making sense of MOOCs: Musings in a maze of myth, paradox and possibility. *Journal of Interactive Media in Education, 2012*(3), Art. 18.

Dennett, D. (2007). Higher games. *The MIT Technology Review.* Retrieved from www.technologyreview.com/s/408440/higher-games/

Deresiewicz, W. (2014). *Excellent sheep: The miseducation of the American elite and the way to a meaningful life.* New York: Free Press.

Descartes, R. (1596–1650/1993). *Discourse on method and Meditations on first philosophy.* Indianapolis: Hackett Pub. Co.

Dewey, J. (1997/1910). *How we think.* New York: Dover.

Levy, S (2014). *"Hackers" and "information wants to be free".* Retrieved from https://medium.com/backchannel/the-definitive-story-of-information-wants-to-be-free-a8d95427641c

Markoff, J. (2011). Computer wins on "Jeopardy!": Trivial, it's not. *The New York Times.* Retrieved from www.nytimes.com/2011/02/17/science/17jeopardy-watson.html

Mozur, P. (2017). Google's alphaGo defeats Chinese go master in win for A.I. *The New York Times.* Retrieved from www.nytimes.com/2017/05/23/business/google-deepmind-alphago-go-champion-defeat.html

Noel, J. (2007). On the varieties of *phronesis. Educational Philosophy and Theory, 31*(3), 273–289.

Pritchard, D. (2018). Neuromedia and the epistemology of education. *Metaphilosophy, 49*, 328–349.

Schrager, A., & Wang, A. (2017). Imagine how great universities could be without all those human teachers. *The Quartz*. Retrieved from https://qz.com/1065818/ai-university/

Searle, J. (1999). The Chinese room. In R. A. Wilson & F. Keil (Eds.), *The MIT encyclopedia of the cognitive sciences*. Cambridge: MIT Press.

Teicher, J. (2018). Garry Kasparov: It's time for humans and machines to work together. *The Medium*. Retrieved from https://medium.com/ibmindustrious/garry-kasparov-its-time-for-humans-and-machines-to-work-together-8cd9e1dc735a

Turing, A. (1950). Computing machinery and intelligence. *Mind, 59*(236), 433–460.

Ubell, R. (2017). How the pioneers of the MOOC got it wrong. *The IEEE Spectrum*. Retrieved from https://spectrum.ieee.org/tech-talk/at-work/education/how-the-pioneers-of-the-mooc-got-it-wrong

Wang, A. (2018). Amazon is quietly becoming its own university. *The Quartz.com*. Retrieved from https://qz.com/1191619/amazon-is-becoming-its-own-university/

Young, J. (2017). Udacity official declares MOOCs 'dead' (Though the company still offers them). *The Edsurge.com*. Retrieved from www.edsurge.com/news/2017-10-12-udacity-official-declares-moocs-dead-though-the-company-still-offers-them.profess

7 Peering Into the F.O.G.

My thesis is that important changes in academic mission are accompanied by structural changes during times of major innovation in higher education. The main structural elements are Finances, Organization, and Governance (F.O.G.)—an apt mnemonic for aspects of institutions that are seldom well understood by the public, much less by the faculty and students who depend on them.

When it comes to organization and finance, higher education is an accomplished mimic; it takes cues from innovations in other sectors and rapidly adapts them to its own purposes. This was true from the beginnings of the modern university, which borrowed heavily from monastic and ecclesiastical organizations, to the latest for-profits that self-consciously strive to emulate the "dot.com" culture. Between these two extremes, the predominant model of colleges and universities over the past 150 years has been an industrial one, designed both to mirror and to support the shift from a rural, agrarian society to an urban and industrial one. Davidson (2017) attributes the transformation in university organization primarily to Charles William Elliot, who, as president of Harvard in the late nineteenth century, introduced new systems of organization and management that were based on the same theories that were coming to dominate business and manufacturing at the time. Efficiency became the holy grail of all organizations, and measurement was the tool of its discovery and management. In the commercial sector, this led to the invention of the assembly line, specialization of labor, vertical integration, and quantitatively trained managers toting stopwatches and clipboards. In academia, the same forces produced specialized academic departments, standardized tests, a professionalized academic management class, and curricula that moved students through a regulated and graduated curriculum, from general studies through professional education. The new doctoral universities established at the end of the nineteenth century, which had the advantage of building their organizations from scratch, took on characteristics of the "trusts" that sought end-to-end control over their businesses. For example, Chicago's William Rainey Harper seems to have taken business lessons from his patron, John D. Rockefeller, in setting out plans for his new institution (Storr, 1966). Rockefeller built Standard Oil as a vertically integrated company that included exploration, discovery, refining, transportation, and sales of petroleum products, all with the goal of maintaining control of the entire production function and maximizing efficiency. Harper was, by all accounts, equally zealous for efficiency and control over both the creation and dissemination of knowledge. Among Harper's innovations, he established a year-round academic quarter system so that the campus would not sit idle in the summer and during long breaks between semesters; he established an academic press within the university as a distribution channel for faculty work; he also incorporated extension and correspondence programs as full departments of the university in order to reach student markets beyond the boundaries of the campus. The new campus was a factory for the creation of knowledge and the headquarters of its distribution through a multi-channel system.

Across both industry and academia, the organization itself became a kind of machine for converting capital to finished products. In the case of universities, the inputs were money and the raw talent of students; the output was graduates who had been certified in narrow specialties that matched the needs of employers. Standardized testing was introduced to identify the most worthy applicants. Curricula were more highly prescribed, and increasingly came under the control of highly specialized academic departments rather than the collective faculty. Academic credentials were earned more by the number of credits amassed (which, in turn, was based on the amount of hours—or "seat time"—spent in class) instead of evidence of knowledge gained. The entire academic experience was reduced to a system of semester units distributed formulaically among the disciplines, with a plurality of them devoted to a "major" area of study. Although college campuses retained some of their dreamy, counter-cultural reputation, by the early part of the twentieth century, the serious work of higher education was to stamp out "organization men" of uniform specifications with all of the precision of a tool and die shop.

Colleges and universities came increasingly to resemble business corporations in other ways as well. For example, economies of scale tend to reward growth, and successful universities during the twentieth century pursued vigorous expansion not just in terms of enrollment, but as operators of ancillary programs from athletics to housing, and managers of ever greater resources of all kinds: human, physical, and financial. The prototypical academic institution in the mid-twentieth century was not a sleepy, ivy-covered, rural campus, but rather it was Clark Kerr's "multiversity" (2001), a vast enterprise encompassing an enormous range of services, from medical research to quasi-professional sports leagues. The presidents of these large, multi-faceted institutions increasingly resembled the CEO's of corporate conglomerates. While university presidents were once the *primus inter pares* among the faculty, their jobs increasingly came to focus on complex management issues and the constant search for capital. The upper levels of university administration took on the look and culture of a corporate C-suite, populated by executives with large staffs who often acquired their skills in previous careers in industry or government. The same management fads that swept through corporate America were eagerly embraced by academic institutions: quality circles, total quality management, re-engineering, supply chain management, strategic planning, etc., championed by many of the same elite consulting firms who worked in business and industry. The jobs of senior university administrators became defined more by a set of management challenges (marketing, budget management, real estate management, investments, public relations, regulatory compliance, labor relations, etc.) than by the pursuit of an educational mission.

My use of the past tense in the preceding two paragraphs is potentially misleading, because the description is largely still true. Indeed, boards of trustees are turning with increasing frequency to presidents from non-academic backgrounds because of a perception that institutions need leaders with management skills comparable to those of industry. The dominant organizational model of higher education has been slow to adapt, and this reality feeds a perception of the industry as bureaucratically bloated and resistant to change. Much of corporate America—though by no means all—has moved on to more flexible and nimble organizational models. Higher education once again needs to mimic innovations in finances, organization, and governance in order to remain relevant and viable.

The Cost Problem

The most persistent criticism of higher education is its rising cost compared to almost every other part of the economy. Between 1980 and 2014, average (nominal) tuition rates grew at three times the rate of the Consumer Price Index, and yet many institutions continue to have trouble making ends meet. Moody's Investor Services, which issues an annual report on the state of higher education as an industry, offered a bearish outlook at the end of 2017: "The annual change in aggregate operating revenue for four-year colleges and universities will soften to about 3.5% and not keep pace with expense growth, which we expect to be almost 4%" (p. 1). Revenues do not seem to keep up with inexorable cost increases, yet the price of education is increasingly seen as a barrier to access for lower and middle-class families whose incomes have stagnated. Critics increasingly wonder publicly if the return on an investment in education is still positive, putting further pressure on universities to keep tuition increases low. Even within many colleges and universities there is growing concern that the business model of higher education is broken.

Commentaries on higher education costs have generally fallen into two camps: Apologists have taken refuge in the Baumol's "cost disease" theory, discussed earlier, which claims that colleges and universities are among a type of organization that cannot reduce costs without a degradation in the quality of their product. To the contrary, as the theory goes, organizations that are heavily labor-intensive will always have cost rises faster than the general economy because they must raise compensation (their largest expense) in real terms (i.e., higher than the rate of inflation) in order to retain personnel. This general theory has been taken as an important explanation of the Higher Education Price Index (HEPI), which tracks industry costs compared to the Consumer Price Index. Between 1980 and 2017, the CPI grew by a factor of eight, while HEPI increased thirteen-fold (Commonfund Institute, 2017 Update). Annual increases in academic costs were higher than consumer costs every year except during the extraordinarily high inflation years of the late 1970s and early 1980s. If the Baumol theory is correct, HEPI is merely confirmation of an intrinsic property of colleges and universities.

Critics of higher education, on the other hand, tend to see cost increases as failures of both management and imagination. On this view, college and university leaders are to blame for not working harder to find innovative solutions to the cost problem by, for example, cutting programs and weeding out inefficiencies. Other critics charge that federal student loan programs and other public subsidies have served as *de facto* price supports for higher education, and have allowed institutions to raise costs without suffering the full effect of a consumer backlash. Still other observers argue that the entire higher education system lacks transparency and accountability, which has enabled colleges and universities to obfuscate the true reasons for cost increases, such as skyrocketing salaries for administrators and faculty and extravagant amenities to attract students from full-pay families. These and other criticisms help to perpetuate a narrative that colleges and universities are unconnected to the hard economic realities with which households and other industries must contend.

A Matter of Alignment

Clark Kerr, the great oracle of higher education in the twentieth century, was once quoted as saying that the three major problems of university administration are "sex for the students, athletics for the alumni, and parking for the faculty" (Time Magazine, 1958). As with all humor, it is the element of truth in this quip that makes it funny. The job of a college or university leader is often best understood as that of a mediator among institutional stakeholders who have competing, and sometimes incompatible interests. None of these stakeholders, however, has a vested interest in efficiency (Bacow, 2017). This fact plays an important causative role in driving up the cost of education, in ways that have seldom been articulated by either the apologists or critics of higher education. The new challenge for college and university administrators is to design organizational and governance structures that better align both internal and external stakeholder interests.

A college or university can be seen as a collection of interest groups, and the larger the institution, the more interest groups will lay claim to some aspect of it. Certain interests exist in some form at virtually all institutions:

- The governing board is the first of these, and ultimately the most powerful. Governing boards are charged with maintaining the long-term health and success of the institution. In practical terms, this means assuring that the institution is well managed by an effective president, and that it observes its financial and regulatory responsibilities. In less specific ways, governing boards are charged with adhering to a founding mission or vision, either as representatives of the public (in the case of public institutions) as fiduciaries of a trust (in the case of private nonprofits), or on behalf of shareholders (in the case of for-profits). Often, the board is strongly influenced by alumni, who have both practical and nostalgic interests in the continuity of the institution.
- In traditional institutions, the faculty make up another large interest group, and by both custom and regulation (as set by accreditors), they play a major role in managing the core academic enterprise. The faculty set academic standards and requirements, oversee the curriculum, and heavily influence the processes of hiring and evaluation within their own ranks.
- Funders represent another, diverse bloc of interests. This includes both federal and state governments, foundations, and donors. In for-profit institutions, this category importantly includes investors. Funding seldom comes without strings attached, and while diversification of revenue sources is healthy for any institution, each successive funding source creates new expectations and, often, obligations.
- Students and their families are another critical interest group, with perhaps the most transactional relationship to the institution. Students expect a variety of services, ranging from academic programs to campus amenities. Many institutions have struggled to remain competitive as prospective students place at least equal emphasis on the quality of living arrangements, recreational facilities, and extra-curricular experiences as on academic programs.

Beyond these interest groups, which exist in one form or another at almost all institutions, cost pressures may also come from the particular circumstances of some campuses. Big time athletic programs, for example, are a phenomenon of large universities and they introduce a range of powerful interests, from superstar coaches to television networks, that demand attention and resources. At all but a handful of institutions, athletic programs cost more than they generate in revenue, but few university presidents would dare suggest that these programs be curtailed for fear of the backlash that would ensue from students, alumni, and the general public.

Amid all of these competing interests, it is difficult for institutional executives to optimize on any single dimension of management. Boards tend to be cautious about making abrupt changes, even if they have the technical authority to approve them. Faculty demand that their professional autonomy be protected from encroachment by non-academics, which makes most attempts to trim programs highly controversial. Outside funders may induce the creation of new activities by offering seed funding, but seldom provide for ongoing support. Students expect ever more choices and services. All of these forces tend to produce expansion. Zemsky, Wegner, & Massy (2005) have called this the "lattice and ratchet" effect. Institutions tend to become more costly both because of increasing complexity (spreading up and out like a lattice), and because costs are ratcheted up each year, as predicted by Baumol's theory.

For all of their similarities to corporate executives, college, and university presidents have comparatively weak executive powers. Despite the fact that they are formally accountable to the board, they must manage by striving for consensus among all stakeholders. Failure to achieve consensus before making large decisions usually means an abrupt, and early, exit for the executive. It is often easier to let the lattice grow, and accommodate the ratcheting up of costs, than it is to face the inevitable confrontations that come from attempts to intervene.

Higher education thus has a particularly challenging form of the agency problem that occurs in other organizations. Until recently, corporate managers in most industries were simply the "hired help" whose incentives were limited to a good salary, occasional expressions of gratitude from company's directors, and a gold watch at retirement. This arrangement provided little incentive for managers to maximize shareholder profits, and so increasingly boards have given senior executives substantial ownership stakes in companies. Stock options and other forms of equity compensation have become widespread in the last three decades (Bebchuck & Fried, 2003), and became especially common among venture capital-backed start-ups in Silicon Valley and elsewhere.

Executive ownership made its appearance in higher education during the heyday of online start-ups in the early 2000s. Venture capitalists entering the field of higher sought to break the model of academic management by empowering presidents, rewarding them for revenue growth and cost efficiencies, and dramatically limiting the influence of other voices, including those of the faculty, students, and accreditors. The model may be said to have succeeded, in that it resulted in the primary outcomes it was designed to produce—rapid growth and large profit margins—at least in the short run. What it failed to do, by most measures, was to produce better academic outcomes.

For all of the ignominy heaped upon for-profit higher education, it is easy to overlook some positive contributions. The theory of accretive change that I have proposed says that innovation in higher education requires new sources of funding. The for-profit experiments of the past two decades opened the door to a source of funding that had not been available to higher education throughout its long history: private capital markets. Arguably, this resource would not have been made available without the use of management incentive structures that help assure investors that institutional managers are aligned with their interests. As both public funding and large-scale philanthropy for higher education have declined, and as market pressures limit tuition increases, private capital be the only potential source of financing for innovation on the horizon. Furthermore, new for-profits have contributed to important innovations, such as the development of online learning platforms, large-scale enrollment management systems, more flexible academic calendars, and new marketing techniques. Most of these innovations have been adopted by mainstream academic institutions, but only after their development had been financed by private interests.

Looking ahead, the dilemma faced by higher education is this: If private capital is the primary source to finance innovation in the future, how can it be harnessed in ways that balance the interests of multiple stakeholders, not just owners and executives? In other words, can we find new ways to reconcile the inherent tensions between money and mission in the academic enterprise?

Corporate Innovation

The modern publicly held corporation is an effective means of organizing capital and talent toward a single purpose: maximizing the financial returns to shareholders. By law, directors, and managers of public companies are obliged to pursue the greatest possible profits available within the bounds of regulation and prudence. Success is defined along a single dimension, and in theory, at least, must not be compromised by non-economic goals.

Therefore, virtually every decision made by a corporate executive must be in service of maximizing shareholder value.

This view of the role of corporations has been criticized for its myopia in the face of other compelling social interests. The pursuit of maximal profits may come at the expense of employees, customers, communities, the environment, and other stakeholders if they are given no consideration in decision-making. Yet the laws governing corporations in most U.S. states offer relatively little leeway for managers to make decisions that are not, at least arguably, in the financial interests of shareholders. Thus, in spite of periodic renewals of interest in business ethics and corporate social responsibility, profit maximization remains the most powerful organizing force in business.

The only alternative to profit-seeking corporations, until recently, has been a not-for-profit organization, which is organized around a religious, social, or philanthropic purpose. It is often assumed that the only difference between the for-profit and nonprofit sectors is their tax status, but this is not the most important distinction. In a not-for-profit structure, all financial resources must be used to pursue the organization's mission. In the event of a surplus, it must be retained for use by the organization rather than distributed in the form of profit back to its source. The line between being an investor, who has expectations of a financial return, and a donor, who can have no such expectation, is absolute. This greatly limits access to capital among not-for-profit organizations, especially among those without a robust donor base. In higher education, the majority of charitable donations go to the wealthiest institutions (Clotfelter, 2017). Philanthropy is an important source of non-operating revenue for a few institutions, but, with a few notable exceptions, it does not provide much fuel for innovation across the large majority of colleges and universities.

In recent years, however, the line between investment and donation has become slightly less absolute. From the philanthropic side, a new generation of large-scale organizations have been created as deliberate hybrids between businesses and charities. These include the Chan-Zuckerberg Initiative and the Emerson Collective, both the products of recent Silicon Valley fortunes (Facebook and Apple, respectively). Both of these organizations encompass a range of charitable grant-making and entrepreneurial activities that are intended to allow greater flexibility in pursuing social goals. From the business side, a growing list of companies are seeking recognition as "B-Corps," a certification of good citizenship and public stewardship that is intended to signal strong public interest commitments on the part of the firm's leadership. These experiments in hybridization reflect a growing dissatisfaction with the stark divide between profit-seeking and social purpose. A new generation of social entrepreneurs has worked to blur the lines between these two realms by seeking to harness the power of capital markets and redirect it toward broader social goods.

These experiments in hybridization between profit-making and social purpose are starting to be recognized in law. In 2010, Maryland became the first state to recognize a modification of its corporate code to create "benefit corporations," and more than thirty other states have since adopted similar legislation (Field, 2013). Generally, a benefit corporation declares one or more goals that are deemed to have positive impact on society, for example to explore alternative energy sources, or to promote health. Investors in the company agree explicitly to support the pursuit of these goals, thereby limiting their claim to maximizing profits. Special accountability rules apply to benefit corporations, requiring them to report regularly not only on their financial performance, but also on the extent to which they have achieved their social purposes. In states with the strongest accountability rules, certain stakeholders can take legal action against benefit corporation managers and directors for failing to achieve positive social outcomes. Thus, the attempt in most benefit corporation regulations is not only to accommodate social goals as a feature of the business, but to require their consideration as a legal obligation in all management decisions.

A Case Study

I became interested in benefit corporations during my time as president of Alliant International University, from 2004 until 2016. I offer my personal experience there as a case study in how the benefit corporation model may serve the purposes of higher education.

Alliant was formed in 2000 from the merger of two older institutions. The California School of Professional Psychology (CSPP) was among the first free-standing schools for training clinical psychologists in the country with headquarters in San Francisco. In an effort to diversify its academic programs, it acquired United States International University (USIU), based in San Diego, and which in its heyday had operated sites in London, Nairobi, and Mexico City. The merged university was not-for-profit, as were its two predecessor institutions. Under the new Alliant name, graduate programs were offered in psychology, education, and business in six California cities and three international locations: Mexico City, Hong Kong, and Tokyo. A small undergraduate program also existed at the former USIU campus in San Diego. In retrospect, there was little to recommend the merger; both institutions were in precarious financial straits, and USIU had struggled to maintain its accreditation. By the time I arrived, in 2004, the combined institution was in serious financial condition and was on the brink of losing its accreditation.

As we have seen, however, institutions of higher education are remarkably resilient. For several years, my colleagues and I worked back toward a fragile equilibrium by reducing expenses, reorganizing programs, and developing a new mission built around professional training. We also made investments in land adjacent to the campus with the idea of leasing it or selling it to provide a new source of income for the institution. The major recession of 2008 disrupted the real estate strategy and soon also began affecting enrollments. Within three or four years, the financial progress we had made was erased; we were running operating deficits and consuming our slender asset base. At the same time, competition from new sources, both for-profit and nonprofit institutions, was putting additional pressure on Alliant to increase investments in marketing, technology, student financial aid, faculty salaries, and facilities.

Alliant needed to modernize and innovate, but there were no resources to finance new initiatives. Debt markets had collapsed during the recession, but Alliant would not have been seen as a good credit risk even in good times. As at most small institutions, annual donations from alumni and others were not substantial enough to make much difference. Raising tuition to generate surplus revenue was neither feasible from a competitive standpoint nor ethical given the levels of debt our students were already incurring. The survival of the institution depended on finding some alternative source of funding.

Several investor groups approached Alliant in those difficult times with proposals to purchase the school and convert it to a for-profit model. Each of them promised infusions of cash to get the institution back on its feet, but each of them also planned to leverage our status as an accredited institution to build out large online programs. Furthermore, the venture capital model always included an "exit strategy"—a point at which the investors could sell the institution at a handsome profit. In most cases, the horizon was less than ten years, at which point the institution would likely be acquired by another owner. This was of concern to everyone who was committed to the long-term future of Alliant, because no matter how committed the initial investors were to maintaining the quality and integrity of the institution, there were no guarantees about future owners. We had seen some of the worst offenses of the for-profit industry and did not want Alliant to become just another example of quality sacrificed in the pursuit of profit.

The benefit corporation model seemed to solve several problems. First, it meant that we could solicit investors, not just donors. New investments would potentially restore the institution's competitiveness by allowing us to invest in much-needed technology and marketing resources, and (finance expansion. We were able to create certain impediments to changing the benefit corporation structure, meaning that even if there was a change of ownership, the University's core commitments would be more difficult to alter. Indeed, the new structure forced greater clarity on our public benefit purposes, and created a structural alignment among investors, the directors and managers of the institution that was based on a shared mission rather than shared financial interests. We enumerated six areas of public benefit to which the institution would be committed:

- Student success, as measured by retention and graduation rates, licensure pass rates, internship, and job placement rates;
- Diversity, as measured by the admission and graduation rates of students representing various kinds of diversity, and the demographics of the faculty and staff;
- Community engagement, as measured by the quantity and impact of community service provided by the students, faculty, and staff;
- Academic quality, as determined by regional and specialized accreditors, awards, and recognition of faculty and student work;
- Student, faculty, and staff satisfaction with the University, as measured by internal surveys;
- Research and scholarship, as measured by scholarly publications and presentations by faculty and students.

In declaring these to be our social purposes in the organizing charter of the new benefit corporation, we assumed legal responsibility for measuring and publicly reporting on them each year. This is potentially a higher standard of accountability than that required even by accreditors and education regulators. Furthermore, it explicitly made faculty, students, and staff the stakeholders and beneficiaries of the institution, which had the potential of assuring that their interests would be reflected in management's decision-making.

Alliant's trustees approved converting the institution to a benefit corporation in 2014, and the transaction was concluded early the next year. It became the first such conversion of a nonprofit institution in American higher education. It was not done without controversy, especially among faculty and students, many of whom were concerned that the loss of independence and nonprofit status would be harmful in the long run. Much of the concern was reputational, since for most public purposes, Alliant would be listed merely as a for-profit institution. It will take time for classification schemes to catch up to the new realities of hybrid organizational models. It will also take time to determine whether the conversion actually achieves its goals.

Alliant's experience cannot be taken as dispositive with respect to the potential for benefit corporations in higher education, but it is one of a growing number of data points. In early 2017, Laureate Education, which owns and operates universities around the world, raised $490 million in an initial public offering as a benefit corporation (Laureate International Universities website, 2017). This was an important ratification of the model in public finance markets, and it paves the way for further experimentation. In a quite different use of the model, Purdue University formed a benefit corporation as a means to acquire Kaplan University, which had been a pioneer in the wave of new for-profit institutions formed in the early 2000s. Benefit corporations may increasingly be seen as offering the best of both worlds between for-profit and nonprofit capital structures (House, 2018).

Other Organizational Reforms

Another area of experimentation in financial and organizational design is to be found in emerging online program management (OPM) industry. As we have seen, online education has dominated discussions of educational innovation for much of the past two decades, and it was greatly advanced by the influx of venture capital into new for-profit institutions. The playbook for many of these online companies was to purchase an accredited traditional college and use it as a platform for launching online programs. This approach bypassed the hurdle of seeking accreditation *de novo*, which takes several years and is a significant barrier to entry for institutions financed on the premise of rapid growth. These acquisitions were not anticipated by accreditors and regulators who, it must be said, were ill-prepared as the number and size of transactions began to increase. Much of the higher education community was aghast at the findings of a Senate investigation led by Iowa Senator Tom Harkin, which documented the extent to which some of these newly converted for-profit institutions had exploited regulatory loopholes and distorted the intent of accreditation (Fain, 2012). In response, both accreditors and the federal government began to tighten restrictions on the acquisition and conversion of accredited institutions, reducing the appeal of this point of entry for investors.

What could no longer be done by acquisition is now increasingly done by contract. OPMS are companies that specialize in creating and marketing online educational programs in partnership with accredited institutions (Hill, 2018a). In a typical model, the OPM fully finances online course development, recruits instructors, markets the program, and operates the infrastructure necessary to enroll and instruct students. This is done in the name and under the aegis of the college or university, which is therefore able to extend its accreditation (and reputation) to the online programs. In theory, the academic institution retains strong oversight of program quality, though in practice the actual degree of involvement from the institution may vary widely. In a typical contract, the OPM retains anywhere from 60 to 80 percent of the revenues generated by the program to recover its costs and make a profit. For the college or university, the promise is a steady stream of income (i.e., the remaining 20 to 40 percent) for which it has not had to make a capital investment or increase operating expenses. One leading market analyst (Hill, 2018b) reports that the OPM industry has become a $1.5 to $2.5 billion industry in the space of just a few years.

As with benefit corporations, OPM arrangements have not been without controversy among traditional academics. In 2014, for example, the California State University system withdrew from a planned partnership (Straumsheim, 2014); in 2015 the University of Florida canceled a large contract and brought its online programs fully in-house (Ibid., 2016); in 2017 the faculty of Eastern Michigan University filed an accreditation complaint against their university's partnership with an OPM (Supiano, 2017). And despite the rapid growth in revenues, it is not clear that the OPM industry is either profitable or sustainable over the long run. For one thing, while some colleges and universities greatly benefit from the availability of investment funds to create online programs, they have little incentive to renew contracts once the programs are established and running and operating costs are relatively low. The value proposition of OPMs for most institutions is relatively short-lived.

That said, OPMs represent a new model of partnership between traditional institutions and the commercial sector. Other partnerships are becoming common in the construction of dormitories, the provision of food services, bookstore management, and the recruitment of international students (a growing and potentially lucrative market for most U.S. colleges and universities). Each of these areas of business typically involves substantial infusions of capital from the company in exchange for a share of operating revenues. These partnerships are especially attractive to undercapitalized institutions that face the greatest challenges in upgrading and innovating their programs, services, and facilities.

Yet another form of innovation that is emerging is one in which traditional institutions become parent companies for both nonprofit and for-profit subsidiaries. Grand Canyon University, which converted from nonprofit to for-profit status and became one of the fastest growing institutions in the country, recently announced that its latest restructuring would involve the creation of two parallel organizations under a single chief executive (McKenzie, 2018). Grand Canyon University, a new nonprofit, will enroll and educate nearly 100,000 online students, while its sister company, Grand Canyon Education, will operate as a for-profit company that will "manage most of the institution's nonacademic operations" (Blumenstyk, 2018) in a multi-year agreement. This arrangement seems primarily intended to allow the combined institution access to *both* philanthropic and investment capital. Another example of a for-profit subsidiary under a traditional structure is Purdue University's acquisition of Kaplan University, mentioned above, which adds yet another creative element to the experiment. As a public university, Purdue is attempting to incorporate a for-profit element within the governance of a state agency.

These and other innovations all point toward a blending of profit-driven and mission-driven organizational cultures, providing more flexible access to capital depending upon the opportunities and constraints of each situation. The good news for academia is that there is a larger trend toward socially responsible capitalism that can be tailored for educational purposes. Further experimentation is inevitable in the coming years.

Conclusion to Part II

The south end of Market Street in downtown San Francisco is a dismal urban landscape filled with sketchy storefronts, transient hotels, and chronic homelessness. The character of the neighborhood is changing rapidly however, as Silicon Valley firms such as Facebook have taken up residence nearby, pushing up rents and gentrifying entire city blocks. South Market Street is also the home of Minerva Schools, which is among the most ambitious current projects aimed at reinventing higher education.

Minerva was founded in 2012 by Ben Nelson, who combines educational idealism with an entrepreneur's bombast. Backed by an initial capital investment of $25 million, Nelson's vision is to create an elite institution that blends online coursework with international residential experiences (McBride, 2013). Cohorts of students live in various settings around the world, connected to the home university through small seminars that meet with instructors by video conference. The curriculum makes critical thinking, problem solving, and communications—a reasonable approximation of the intellectual arts as described above—the explicit educational objective rather than an accidental byproduct of the traditional liberal arts approach (Fain, 2018). Minerva's organization and finances blur the traditional boundaries between for-profit and nonprofit by housing both under a single institutional umbrella. The nonprofit side of the house administers the educational program and grants degrees, while a parallel for-profit structure focuses on technology development that can be sold to other institutions. By avoiding large fixed costs, including traditional campuses, Minerva leaders aim to keep nominal tuition low compared to virtually all other private institutions.

Minerva has also challenged the flexibility of the accrediting system, while still operating within it. New institutions are generally required to operate for several years in order to prove that they can meet accreditation standards. This is both a high barrier to entry, and something of a Catch-22. Typically, a new unaccredited institution must attract students and even graduate an initial class in order to show that it is worthy of accreditation. Minerva worked around this barrier by creating a partnership with the Keck Graduate Institute (KGI), which is part of the Claremont consortium of colleges in southern California. In theory, Minerva's academic programs are an extension of KGI's, with the latter providing substantial oversight. This provides justification for including Minerva's programs under KGI's accreditation until the day when Minerva can become accredited in its own right. In reality, the oversight is a polite fiction, which the accreditor has allowed to persist in order to accommodate an innovative experiment. Minerva's programs have nothing to do with KGI's curriculum, its methods of delivery, or its faculty governance, and nothing suggests that KGI has either the competence or the means to direct Minerva's affairs. The WASC Senior College and University Commission—the relevant accreditor—could have stood in the way of this arrangement and forced Minerva to earn accreditation the hard way. Instead, it has extended the benefit of the doubt to an institution that appears to be a well-intentioned, educationally sound experiment.

In short, Minerva manifests virtually all of the marks of accretive change that I have described throughout this book. It also may portend the emergence of a new model for higher education with respect to academic purpose, organization, and finance. Minerva correctly, in my view, has identified a key academic mission that is, if not entirely novel, a restatement of educational goals that will become increasingly important in the coming infosphere. Minerva has created a substantially new business model that blends elements of both for-profit and nonprofit structures. It has been financed by an unusual combination of investments, donations, and alternative revenue streams. The traditional academy, as represented by the accreditation system, far from trying to shut down a nascent competitor, has bent its own rules to accommodate an innovative start-up. If Minerva is successful, it will not be because it beats Harvard at its own game, its founder's frequent public boasts notwithstanding. It will because it has established itself as yet another alternative model that will add to the diversity of the higher education enterprise—and influence the course of evolution for the entire industry.

Bibliography

Bacow, L. (2017). The political economy of cost control on a university campus. *Clark Kerr Lecture.* Video available on University of California Television. Retrieved from www.uctv.tv/shows/The-Political-Economy-of-Cost-Control-on-a-University-Campus-32375

Baumol, W. J., & Bowen, W. G. (1966). *Performing arts, the economic dilemma: A study of problems common to theater, opera, music, and dance.* Cambridge: MIT Press.

Bebchuck, L., & Fried, J. (2003). *Executive compensation as an agency problem.* John M. Olin Center for Law, Business, and Economics, Harvard University. Retrieved from www.law.harvard.edu/programs/olin_center/papers/pdf/421.pdf

Blumenstyk, G. (2018). Grand Canyon U. isn't just becoming a nonprofit: It's also testing a model that could change higher ed. *The Chronicle of Higher Education.* Retrieved from www.chronicle.com/article/Grand-Canyon-U-Isn-t-Just/243826

Clotfelter, C. (2017). How rich universities get richer. *The Chronicle of Higher Education.* Retrieved from www.chronicle.com/article/How-Rich-Universities-Get/241567

Commonfund Institute. (2017). *Commonfund higher education price index: 2017 update.* Retrieved from www.commonfund.org/wp-content/uploads/2017/12/2017-HEPI-Report.pdf

Davidson, C. N. (2017). *The new education: How to revolutionize the university to prepare students for a world In flux.* New York: Basic Books.

Fain, P. (2012). Results are in. *The Inside Higher Ed.* Retrieved from www.insidehighered.com/news/2012/07/30/harkin-releases-critical-report-profits

Fain, P. (2018). A curriculum to copy? *The Inside Higher Ed.* Retrieved from www.insidehighered.com/digital-learning/article/2018/12/05/minerva-project-draws-notice-its-practical-rigorous-curriculum

Field, A. (2013). First-ever study of Maryland benefit corps released. *The Forbes.* Retrieved from www.forbes.com/sites/annefield/2013/01/25/first-ever-study-of-maryland-benefit-corps-released/#4c6d31405e80

Hill, P. (2018a). A look at the OPM market, spring, 2018. *E-Literate.* Retrieved from https://mfeldstein.com/online-program-management-market-landscape-s2018/?utm_source=e-Literate+Newsletter&utm_medium=email&utm_campaign=2c38c19e86-RSS_EMAIL_CAMPAIGN&utm_term=0_deab6fbf84-2c38c19e86-40282373

Hill, P. (2018b). OPM market may be growing, but it's not without chaos. *Education Dive.* Retrieved from https://mfeldstein.com/opm-market-may-be-growing-but-its-not-without-chaos/

House, J. (2018). Are college benefit corporations a new model for higher ed? *Education Dive.* Retrieved from www.educationdive.com/news/are-college-benefit-corporations-a-new-model-for-higher-ed/515925/

Kerr, C. (2001). *The uses of the university.* Cambridge: Harvard University Press. Retrieved from www.jstor.org/stable/j.ctt6wpqkr

Laureate International Universities website. (2017). *Laureate Education, Inc., the first public benefit corporation to go public, is named "B Corp MVP" in 2017.* Retrieved from www.laureate.net/newsroom/pressreleases/2017/10/bcorpmvp2017

McBride, S. (2013). Entrepreneur starts his vision of Harvard, tuition free. *Reuters.* Retrieved from www.reuters.com/article/us-usa-education-minerva/entrepreneur-starts-his-version-of-harvard-tuition-free-idUSBRE98G07620130917

McKenzie, L. (2018). Grand Canyon's OBM business takes shape. *The Inside Higher Ed.* Retrieved from www.insidehighered.com/news/2018/12/19/grand-canyon-universitys-opm-business-gets-ground-focus-health-care

Moody's Investors Service, & Financial Information Services. (2017). *2018 outlook changed to negative as revenue growth moderates*. New York: Moody's Investors Service. Retrieved from www.insidehighered.com/sites/default/server_files/medi a/2018OutlookforHigherEducationChangedtoNegative.pdf

Storr, R. J. (1966). *Harper's university: The beginnings: A history of the university of Chicago*. Chicago: University of Chicago Press.

Straumsheim, C. (2014). Shrinking cal state online. *The Inside Higher Ed*. Retrieved from www.insidehighered.com/news/2014/07/22/california-state-u-system-nixes-online-degree-arm-shared-services-model

Straumsheim, C. (2016). The guesswork of going online. *The Inside Higher Ed*. Retrieved from www.insidehighered.com/news/2016/05/19/2u-hopes-lower-risk-program-selection-algorithm

Supiano, B. (2017). Faculty members at one more university push back at online programs. *The Chronicle of Higher Education*. Retrieved from www.chronicle. com/article/Faculty-Members-at-One-More/241788

Time Magazine. (1958, November 17). *Education: View from the bridge*. New York: Time Inc. Retrieved from http://content.time.com/time/magazine/article/ 0,9171,810691,00.html

Zemsky, R., Wegner, G., & Massy, W. (2005). *Remaking the American university: Market-smart and mission-centered*. New Brunswick, NJ: Rutgers University Press.

Afterword

The late theologian Jarislov Pelikan wrote, "All too often lacking in studies of the university as *institution*, is a consideration of the university as *idea*" (1992, p. 24). In this book I have treated colleges and universities almost entirely as institutions: political, managerial, and financial entities that are shaped by social and economic forces with which they have no choice but to conform if they are to survive. But what of the noble ideas that first led to the establishment of universities, and which remain their nominal reason for being? Is it possible to remain aspirational in the analysis of higher education?

Organizational theorists (Bourgeois, 1984; March, 1991) have long debated the extent to which institutional change is reactive and deterministic, or, alternatively, the product of rational choices made by leaders and managers. Having relied on a theory of organizational ecology in this book, I may seem to be committed to the determinist's camp. As in evolutionary theory, we seem to be led to the realization that we and our organizations are merely the contingent outcomes of blind forces far beyond our control. On this theory, it is illusory to think that the aspirations of institutional leaders have much, if anything, to do with the evolution of their organizations.

The question of determinism in organizations is analogous to the classic problem of free will at the individual level, and is amenable to the same kind of compatibilist resolution that is now in vogue among philosophers (Wolf, 1990; Fisher, 2006). We are free to act on our motivations and intentions, but only within a set of feasible alternatives that are constrained by our condition as physical and temporal beings. Freedom, according to this view, is the ability to choose among alternatives in ways that are consistent with prior commitments and values. Indeed, it is the presence of such commitments and values that enable us to be free. Choice is only meaningful if it is to serve some purpose, and purpose only makes sense if it is consistent and enduring.

Universities arose to support intellectual interaction, first between teachers and students, and increasingly among colleagues engaged in a complex mix of education, research, and public service. Although the forms and means for accomplishing these purposes have changed over time, institutions of higher education have been characterized by a remarkably stable set of preferences: For inquiry over dogma; for openness over secrecy; for merit over privilege. Of course these preferences have not always been honored to the fullest extent, and at times they have been ignored altogether. "Choices are often made without much regard for preferences." (March, op. cit., p. 99). The ongoing challenge of college and university leaders is to live up to their own rhetoric.

I have argued in this book that higher education consistently rises to the challenges presented to it. This is not the result of blind socio-economic forces, but rather it is the legacy of educators who have been committed to the continuity of certain ideals. The means by which they have pursued this commitment – the feasible set of alternatives available to them – have changed dramatically as a result of technology, the economy, and evolving cultural norms, and it is in this sense that social ecology constrains outcomes. The contours of the river change, but it continues to flow toward its destination.

Inherent in the idea of higher education is that it not be merely swept along with the current, however. The larger purposes of education should take priority over the vagaries of time and place. Thus, the moral commitments to expand access, to assure equity, to educate effectively, to honor diversity of opinion, and to conduct research with integrity should not be compromised because they are difficult in these times. Losing sight of these fundamental goals would be to cut the through line of higher education's history, and imperil its future.

Bibliography

Bourgeois III, L. (1984). Strategic management and determinism. The academy of management review (9)(4) 586–596.

Fisher, J. (2006). *My Way*, New York: Oxford University Press

March, J. (1991). How decisions happen in organizations. *Human-computer interaction* (6) 95–117.

Pelikan, J. (1992). *The idea of the university: A reexamination.* New Haven: Yale University Press.

Wolf, S. (1990). *Freedom within Reason*, Oxford: Oxford University Press

Index

Printed in the United States
by Baker & Taylor Publisher Services